AN IRISH MOMENT

'I am the wind which breathes upon the sea,
I am the wave of the ocean,
I am the murmur of the billows,
I am the ox of the seven combats,
I am the vulture of the rocks,
I am the beam of the sun,
I am the fairest of plants,
I am a wild boar in valour,
I am a salmon in the water,
I am a lake in the plain,
I am a word of science,
I am the point of a lance of battle,
I am the God who creates in the head the fire …'

(From the Mystery of Amergin, the first known poetry
composed in Ireland, translated from the
Irish by Professor Kuno Meyer 1858-1919)

The Publishers wish to express their gratitude to the Irish Tourist Board
and the Northern Ireland Tourist Board for supplying many of the photographs
featured in this book.

Text and captions
Terence Sheehy

Photography
Bord Failte – Irish Tourist Board
Northern Ireland Tourist Board
The Slide File, Dublin
Colour Library Books Ltd

Commissioning
Trevor Hall
Andrew Preston

Editorial
Fleur Robertson
Gill Waugh

Production
Gerald Hughes
Ruth Arthur
Joanna Keywood

Director of Publishing
David Gibbon

CLB 2156
© 1989 Colour Library Books Ltd, Godalming, Surrey, England.
All rights reserved.
Printed in Italy.
Published in 1989 by Portland House, a division of dilithium Press, Ltd,
distributed by Crown Publishers, Inc, 225 Park Avenue South,
New York, New York 10003.
ISBN 0 517 65936 0
h g d e d c b a

AN IRISH
MOMENT

Terence J. Sheehy

PORTLAND HOUSE

Top right: a Dublin street scene, and (top left) Ulster Folk Museum, Co. Down. There is only one warning for the unsuspecting tourist – never underestimate the man leaning up against the village shop front (above) with his bicycle. He may be a 'returned Yank' who has spent a lifetime in America.

'When God made Time, he made plenty of it', says an old Irish adage. 'An Irish moment', therefore, can last for as little as a fleeting second or as long as a hundred years in the Emerald Isle.

A life-time study of Irish moments, in particular those of Saint Patrick, was begun in days and nights when I warmed the benches in the history lecture halls of the National University of Ireland in Dublin. From my tutors then, and since, I learnt of the greatness of the Gael in re-Christianising the Europe of the Dark Ages. In working and travelling extensively for a number of years throughout the United States and Canada, I met Irish exiles hungry for news of the Celtic, the Patrician and the Golden Days of the Mother Land, a desire to learn about the country of their roots.

I have followed the many paths that Saint Patrick trod in Ireland, Wales and France. I have sailed in a small twelve-foot boat with a square sail in the wake of the Apostle of Ireland, navigating as he did the waters of the east coast of Ireland, past the hill of Howth and Rogerstown, through the narrows of Lambay Island, and on to Skerries, landing on Saint Patrick's Island, as he did, and then sailing on past the Mountains of Mourne through the narrow straits to the waters of Strangford Lough, to the mouth of the Slaney River, where Saint Patrick landed at Saul, two miles from where he had herded swine as a slave boy.

I have flown low over Tara and Royal Meath and on to Derry, looking down on the green fields of his apostolic labours. Twice I have gone on pilgrimage, fasting days and nights and doing penance on Lough Derg, in County Donegal, Saint Patrick's Purgatory. I have climbed 'The Reek', Croagh Patrick, Patrick's mountain above the shores of Clew Bay. Here the Apostle of Ireland fasted for forty days and forty nights, wresting from the Lord the right to judge the Irish on the Last Day. And I have followed in the footsteps of the early Irish monk-missionaries throughout Britain and on through France, Italy and Austria and much of the rest of Europe.

Special as they all are, perhaps the most precious moments in Irish history occurred during these heroic journeyings of the Irish saints in the Dark Ages, when the Gael was responsible for re-Christianising Europe. With little but their love of God and learning, Irish monks went forth from Ireland and, against all the odds and with great risk to their own lives, brought the Word of God to the barbarian tribes that had overrun the Continent. It is largely this Irish contribution to European history that I consider in *An Irish Moment* – a magical time of Celtic ascendancy that produced some of the country's finest literary and artistic achievements.

I have found that time appears to stand still in Ireland, and that sundials on the west coast are precisely twenty minutes slower than those in the gardens of the Royal Observatory on the banks of the Thames in Greenwich in England, where the nought meridian sets the time zones of the world.

The Irish poet and writer, Dr Oliver St John Gogarty, with whom I have had many a convivial literary lunch in New York, used to say, at the port or brandy stage, 'Gyroscope yourself up into a region of calm, into the Fourth Dimension'. So it is in *An Irish Moment*, through which we are carried up into the time warp of the Fourth Dimension in the land of Tir na n'Og, the land of Eternal Youth, the Never-Never Land.

For sure, Father O'Time waits for no man as he scythes his way through the precious moments of the comings and goings of the Irish race. However, it is said that on all flights from Britain to Belfast today he nudges the captain to remind the passengers to set their watches back by exactly three hundred years.

The Irish poet Dr Oliver St John Gogarty had a timeless tale to tell of Irish moments. He was once, God rest him, a passenger on a local rural bus going to Connemara in the west of Ireland in torrential rain. He turned to a farmer seated beside him and remarked, 'It is most extraordinary weather for this time of year'.

The old man in the navy-blue serge suit replied, 'Ah, it isn't this time of year at all'.

As the Doctor wrote in his subsequent book, he was evidently in the Fourth Dimension, as are we all in *An Irish Moment*.

'The land is fruitful and rich in its fertile soil and plentiful harvests.
Crops abound in the fields, flocks on the mountains, and wild animals
in the woods. The island is, however, richer in pastures than in crops,
and in grass than in grain. The crops give great promise in
the blade, even more in the straw, but less in the ear.
The island is rich in pastures and meadows, honey and milk.'

(Giraldus Cambrensis 1146-1223)

☐
The River Bride (right) is
associated with 42,000
acres once owned by the
Elizabethan adventurer,
Sir Walter Raleigh. Below:
Garrane Standing Stones,
part of a prehistoric fort
near Crookstown.

□
Right: the colours of the surf and sea are mirrored in the roofs and walls of crofts near Mizen Head, Ireland's southwesterly tip, which points like a finger out into the turbulent waters of the Atlantic Ocean. Below: the Caha Mountains and (below right) Knocknagallaun.

Hibernia, Insula Sanctorum et Doctorum, Ireland, Island of Saints and Scholars, was the title the Irish missionary monks won for their country during the sixth and seventh centuries. This period in the history of Ireland has been hailed as its Golden Age, the 'Irish miracle'. At this time, wave after wave of learned, truly humble and holy Irish monks felt compelled to become *peregrini*, or 'wanderers for Christ'. Such had been the total success of the conversion of the pagan Celtic Irish to Christianity by Saint Patrick that the people of Ireland had not only accepted the teachings of Christ, but had also shown an astounding enthusiasm to share their newly found faith with the pagans of Europe. Schooled in their monastic universities, the monks set out in large numbers to convey the Christian message back into Europe, which, after the fall of Rome, had been overrun by Goths, Vandals and Huns.

Below and bottom: a summer afternoon on a farm in the Baltimore district (left).

To understand these men, first one must understand the Ireland the great Saint Patrick, who started it all, found upon his arrival. This country never saw the Roman eagle or heard the tramp of Roman legions – indeed, it seems clear from the *Agricola* of the Roman historian Tacitus that the Romans did not know where Ireland lay. There was a vague notion that she was between Spain and Britain, somewhere near Iceland. It was not until AD 82 – a century after the Roman invasion of Britain – that Agricola, moving west along the Solway Firth in Ayrshire, looked across at Ireland and thought of invading it.

Says Tacitus, who was married to Julius, the daughter of Agricola, Roman ruler of Britain, and was writing in AD 98, 'I have often heard Agricola say that Ireland could be reduced and held by a single legion with a fair-sized

The Beara Peninsula (above) is the most westerly of the many
long fingers of land in County Cork that thrust into the Atlantic. It
stretches over thirty miles in length and lies between Bantry Bay
and the Kenmare River estuary.

☐ Cork city (right) is set in the largest of the thirty-two counties of Ireland and its charming people are great lovers of mime and literature. Above: a horse fair at Buttervant.

force of auxiliaries; and that it would be easier to hold Britain if it were completely surrounded by Roman armies, so that liberty was banished from its sight.'

The strength of a legion was about 5,000 men. Considering that Britain could not be held in subjection by the governor, Agricola, with an occupation force of four legions, and their auxiliary forces, the Romans vastly underestimated the size of the force which they would have have required to invade and occupy Ireland. In general, the Romans were crassly ignorant of the place. Not only did they not know where it was but their secondhand descriptions of it vaguely referred to its 'green fields', and to its being 'the Sacred Isle.' That renowned fourth-century Biblical scholar, Saint Jerome, has not endeared himself to the Irish people by his

☐
This page: village streets and shops in County Cork that have not changed much during the past century.

Left: a rainbow shields the Father Mathew Memorial Church and Parliament Bridge, which crosses the River Lee (bottom) in the city of Cork (below).

outrageous observation that the inhabitants of the Emerald Isle were cannibals, who delighted in eating the more delectable parts of the female form. One Roman historian, Diodorus Siculus, writing in the first century before Christ, had this to say about the Celts:

'Physically the Celts are terrifying in appearance with deep-sounding and very harsh voices. In conversation they use few words and speak in riddles, for the most part hinting at things and leaving a great deal to be understood. They frequently exaggerate with the aim of extolling themselves and diminishing the status of others. They are boasters and threateners, and given to bombastic self-dramatization, and yet they are

☐
The City Hall (right) of
Cork, which stands
beside the south channel
of the River Lee (below),
is a modern building of
domes and columns
crowned by a chiming
bell tower. The spacious
Assembly Hall can
accommodate 2,000

people. Cork (remaining
pictures), the third
largest city in Ireland, is a
university city famous for
its medieval school.

☐
Cork was founded in the sixth century by St
Finbarr. He built a church on the south bank
of the River Lee (right).

□
Right: a snow-soaked
Saint Patrick's Day
Parade in Cork is
brightened by a host of
little girls in yellow
dresses and black
boleros.

□
Above: a small, but
brightly coloured,
shopfront in Cork, and
(right) sunset
silhouetting the city's
Protestant Cathedral of
St Finbarr. This is said to
occupy the site of the
sixth-century church of
the saint, who founded
the city.

Inchydony (below), west Cork, lies just three miles from
Clonakilty and boasts a fine sandy beach. Clonakilty is famous as
the birthplace of the Irish leader Michael Collins, who was born in
a farmhouse near the town.

quick of mind and with a good-natured ability for learning. They have also
lyric poets whom they call Bards. They sing to the accompaniment of
instruments resembling lyres, sometimes a eulogy and
sometimes a satire.'

The Irish Celtic warrior was a fierce fighter, who flung himself naked into
battle, wearing only his helmet, a neck torque and belt, and carrying a
small, bronze spear or short, stabbing sword. To the Romans and the
Greeks the fighting Celt was an awesome sight. A Greek geographer of the
late first century before Christ, Strabo, said of the Celts:

'At any time or place, you will find them ready to face danger, even if they
have nothing on their side but their own strength and courage.'

The pre-Roman Celtic civilisation stretched right across Europe from
Ireland, including the Pyrenees and the River Rhine, as far as Romania.
When the Roman legions withdrew to protect Rome in the fifth century,
the Celts moved in to fill the gap. Celtic Europe flourished between the
sixth and seventh centuries before Christ, until the second century B.C.
When Britain fell to the Romans, the Irish were ruled by an exotic
aristocracy of chieftains, Druids, bards and law-makers with their own
distinctive Celtic language and culture. As one historian put it:

'Celtic heritage is no mean tradition – they have beauty in decorative art
and lyric poetry, imagination in literature, devotion to ideals rather than to
material gain. They have vitality and a will to survive, and courage in

Above: a cottage window. One of the grandest sights is an Irish
window on Christmas Eve, when it is traditional to place a candle
there to give guiding light to the Mother of God on her way to the
stable in Bethlehem.

☐
Below: a landscape near Kinsale, which used to be one of the chief ports of the British Navy. Right: a Cork churchyard and (bottom) the Sheehy Mountains.

battle. When St Patrick asked Caoilte in the Colloquy, "What maintained you so in your lives?", Caoilte replied "Truth in our hearts, strength in our arms and fulfillment in our tongues".'

Ancient Celtic Ireland was divided into the Four Provinces of Ulster, Connacht, Munster and Leinster, and its pagan inhabitants were conscious of the importance of the intellect and the soul, and had an intense appreciation the beautiful things of nature. They were profoundly moved by the cry of a seagull, the leap of a salmon, the silence of the forests, the roar of the Atlantic ocean and the movements of the sun, the moon and the stars.

Right: Adrigole Bay. For
many people the real
scenic glory of this
county lies in the west, in
the long arms of land
reaching out into the
Atlantic Ocean against
their backdrop of
spectacular mountain
ranges (below).

The earliest inhabitants of Ireland probably settled on the west coast six
thousand years before the birth of Christ. They built stone tombs over
their dead leaders whose capstones weighed many tons. They dug great
tomb-chambers, and carved ornately decorated passage graves – those at
Newgrange, Dowth and Knowth in County Meath were built before the
pyramids of Egypt. They were craftsmen in bronze and gold, creating
ornaments such as torcs, gorgets and lunulae. The earliest Celtic designs
are in the La Tène style, the best extant example being the Turoe Stone in
County Galway. The high king of the Celts and his court were established
on the Hill of Tara in County Meath, near where Saint Patrick lit the
Paschal fire on the Hill of Slane and brought the first light of
Christianity to Ireland.

☐ This page: Blarney Castle. The word 'blarney' took its place in the English language after 1602. Cormac Macarthy, the then Lord of Blarney, managed, by means of his wheedling speeches, to avoid swearing allegiance to Carew, Queen Elizabeth's deputy, for so long that the deputy became the laughing stock of the county, and such clever excuses became known as 'blarney'. Bottom: kissing the Blarney Stone to obtain the gift of eloquence.

Saint Patrick is one of the best known saints of the Christian world, as is evidenced by the fact that over two thousand cathedrals and churches are dedicated to his name. The home cathedral is Saint Patrick's in Dublin, which stands just outside the walls of the original city and is associated with a holy well of Saint Patrick. The present cathedral was built largely by the Anglo-Normans and dedicated to Saint Patrick on 17th March 1192. A Benedictine monk, John Cummin, was appointed Archbishop of Dublin. He died in 1212, and a bosom companion of the 'Bad' King John of England, Henry de Loundres, was then enthroned, and raised the church to the status of a cathedral. The Guinness family – they of the black stout reported to be good for you – 'restored' the cathedral between 1860 and 1864, hence its rather heavy, Victorian edifice. Today, the cathedral is perhaps most famous for its eighteenth-century dean, Jonathan Swift, the

Left: Kinsale, a port of great beauty, where William Penn was once Clerk of the Admiralty Court. Top: Glandore and (above) Mizen Head.

Top: Fastnet Rock, which lies four miles southwest of Cape Clear, is aptly known in Irish as 'Carraig Aonair' – the Lone Rock. Its tall, white lighthouse is a landmark for yachtsmen and transatlantic sailors. Top right: the harbour at Cobh, near Cork, on Great Island. Above: Dromberg Stone Circle and (left) the view from Goats Path overlooking the Beara Peninsula.

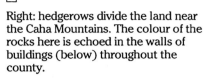

Right: hedgerows divide the land near the Caha Mountains. The colour of the rocks here is echoed in the walls of buildings (below) throughout the county.

Above right: a stained glass window in Bantry House, built in 1750. This was once the home of the Earl of Bounty and houses many historic treasures, such as tapestries and furniture, and some *objets d'art* that once belonged to Marie Antoinette. Right: ruined fortifications softened by grass.

satirical author of *Gulliver's Travels*. This mightily disturbed man died in 1745 and is buried in the cathedral near his beloved Stella. A brass plate marks his grave. On the nearby south wall is a bust of him, and one can read his well-known epitaph, written by himself, above one of the doorways:

'Here is laid the body of Jonathan Swift, Doctor of Divinity, Dean of this Cathedral Church, where fierce indignation can no longer rend the heart. Go, traveller, and imitate, if you can, this earnest and dedicated champion of liberty. 1745 AD. Aged 78 years.'

Profit from the sale of alcohol played a major part in restoring the ancient churches of Dublin – Guinness restored Saint Patrick's Cathedral, and Henry Roe, an Irish whiskey distiller and millionaire, did the same for Christ Church Cathedral which stands on the hill above the River Liffey, and was founded in 1038.

After Dublin's, New York City's Saint Patrick's Cathedral is the best known. It was built largely on the dimes and cents of immigrant Irish servant girls who slaved 'below stairs' in the mansions of the millionaires of Wall Street. The history of Saint Patrick's Cathedral, New York, is very much part of the history of the entrepreneurial spirit which made the United States so great. The site was originally a few rocky fields at the end of a dusty country road, but Archbishop Hughes had the vision to see that this patch of rural estate, then considered a little too far from New York City, would one day stand in the heart of the city. When the Civil War ended

The Earl of Bantry, who built Bantry House (above), was arguably of the family of plain Mr White. In 1796, Richard White gave information about the French invasion to the British and was made a baron for his services. He was later to become a viscount and then an earl – the Earl of Bantry.

□

Right: Lough Acoose in Macgillycuddy's Reeks and (below) perfect reflections in a lough in the 'Ring of Kerry'. Facing page: sheep and stones in the Black Valley.

the walls were only a few feet high. The Cathedral was dedicated in 1879, having been completed by America's first cardinal, John McCloskey.

Saint Patrick's Cathedral, Melbourne was built on sheep lands leased from the Crown in the 1840s by Edward Curr, an English Catholic. The building was begun in 1858 and the cathedral was dedicated in 1897. On the other side of the world, Saint Patrick's Cathedral in Montreal was dedicated in 1847. The first Irish immigrants had come to Montreal, in the French-speaking province of Quebec, around 1817. The architect of the Canadian cathedral was a Jesuit, Fr Martin. After a succession of able Irish-born priests – Fr Dowd, Fr, O'Brien and Fr McCullough – the first native-born Canadian pastor, Fr John Joseph Patrick Quinlivan, was appointed to St Patrick's in 1878. He was born in Stratford, Ontario and he more than any other man is responsible for the magnificently rich interior of the Cathedral as it stands today.

'There grows the wild ash; and a time-stricken willow
Looks chidingly down on the mirth of the billow,
As, like some gay child that sad monitor scorning,
It lightly laughs back to the laugh of the morning.'

(J.J. Callanan 1795-1829)

☐
Above and facing page bottom right: a Dingle shepherd and (right) part of his flock. The men and women of the 'Kingdom of Kerry' are among the best-looking and most articulate people in Ireland. In the main, they are mountain dwellers who retain their Gaelic culture – and a certain aloofness too.

☐
Right and below: Kerry hill farms. Bottom: Caherconree Mountain, one of the highest in Kerry's Slieve Mish range.

The national Apostle of Ireland, universally accepted throughout Christendom as a saint, and with over two thousand cathedrals and churches to his name, is an accepted historical figure, as historically true as George Washington or Winston Churchill. We possess two works penned by his own hand, his *Confession* and his *Letter to the Soldiers of Coroticus*. His *Confession* is akin to Cardinal Newman's *Apologia Pro Vita Sua*. While the Cardinal, a classical scholar and intellectual genius, wrote in superb English, Patrick wrote in dictated and primitive Latin. Nevertheless, he revealed himself in these works as a supremely humble but highly complex character, a man close to the Bible and to the writings of great doctors of the church, such as those of Saint Jerome. Here he also defended himself from his ecclesiastical detractors, giving an overall view of his unique form of work as a missionary. The latter is deserving of

☐

Right: Lough Acoose in Macgillycuddy's Reeks and (below) one of the Killarney lakes. Killarney, 'Heaven's Reflex', has been known for two hundred years to tourists as one of the most beautiful lake and mountain districts in Ireland. In some places the lakes are surrounded by dense woods of oak, birch, mountain ash and holly.

particular note because he chose to adopt a direct approach to a purely pagan people, whereas his contemporary bishops were more concerned in their missionary work with their own folk, the already established Christian peoples. By comparison, his *Letter* was written in the white heat of rage at a dastardly attack on his newly converted young men and women, still in their white robes as neophytes, fresh from the waters of baptism, who were carried off by the Welsh-Briton, Chieftain Coroticus and his slave-raiding party. The unfortunate young men were carried into slavery from Ireland to Britain, while the young girls were sold to the brothels of Europe.

More precious than the Book of Kells, valued at £40 million, is the Book of Armagh, which contains, in the exquisite hand of the scribe, Ferdomnach, the writings of Saint Patrick. Ferdomnach, a scribe of Armagh, penned one of the greatest Irish manuscripts ever known. Despite its being over a 1,180 years old, it is perfectly legible, looking for all the world as if it had

☐

Left: the shore of
Glanmore Lake in the
Slieve Miskish range.
Above: a laden signpost
near Moll's Gap, and
(below) the wooded
slopes of Macgillycuddy's
Reeks.

☐

Left: Lough Barfinnihy at the foot of Mount Boughil and
(above) typically breathtaking Killarney scenery.

□

Right: the banks of the Kenmare River. Kenmare will be forever associated with Valentine Castlerosse, Earl of Kenmare, who was responsible for establishing one of the most spectacular golf courses in Killarney.

□

Above: the monastery at Skellig Michael and (above right) fishing boats in busy Dingle Harbour. The Dingle Peninsula (right) is the most northerly of the county's mountain promontories and is a Gaelic-speaking area.

Below: cliffs rear up against the might of the Atlantic at Doon
Point, near the mouth of the Shannon River.

been written but yesterday, and anyone with even the most elementary
knowledge of Latin can follow the beautiful script. Ferdomnach's copy of
the writings of Saint Patrick is but once removed from the autograph copy
of Saint Patrick himself. The Latin of Patrick is spoken Latin, not written
Latin, and to the classical scholar appears rather rough and elementary.
This fits in with the fact that, as Patrick was captured by raiding Irish
pirates, along with thousands of others at the age of sixteen, he missed
much of his formal education. Afterwards, as a slave for six years to his
pagan master, educational opportunities were few and far between. All his
life Patrick was terribly conscious of this lack of education and
declares himself:

'What I had to say had to be translated into a tongue foreign to me, as can
be easily proved by the savour of my writing, which betrays how little
instruction and training I have had in the art of words.'

His native tongue, as a Roman Briton from Wales, would have been Celtic-
British, which he was obliged to translate into his rough-and-ready Latin.
The orator Patrick would have been very conscious that his word,
obviously dictated to his secretary-scribe, could never fully convey the
tone of his oratory. He was a very humble man, deeply aware of his own
educational shortcomings, and knew that he was addressing himself not
only to the Irish, who had their own cultured Gaelic language, but to all
those well-educated churchmen, accomplished Latin scholars and
speakers in Britain, France and Rome. Of those he wrote that they had:

◻ Killorghin is the site of the annual three-day 'Puck Fair' (this page) in August, when a goat is placed in an open case, carried through the town and then set down in the middle of the square. The fair is pagan in origin.

□

The town of Dingle (this page) boasts one of the finest seafood restaurants in Ireland, and one of the best-stocked book shops. The town was the headquarters of sundry American film actors during the filming of *Ryan's Daughter*.

'… thoroughly imbibed law and sacred Scripture and never had to change from the language of their childhood days, but were able to make it still more perfect.'

If we study the Latin versions of his two writings, his *Confession* and the *Letter*, we will see that, though Patrick claimed not to be a scholar, he was a man thoroughly acquainted with the Bible – there are nearly two hundred biblical quotations in his writings.

The primary source of the basic version of the *Confession* and of the *Letter* of Patrick in the Book of Armagh has been filled out in the full text of a master copy of both brought to Péronne by Saint Fursey in the seventh century. Patrician scholars are still turning up fragments of illuminated manuscripts in Europe today, all of which help to confirm the authenticity of the original manuscripts of Saint Patrick. The exquisite manuscript on vellum of the Book of Armagh, after many vicissitudes, was bought for £300 in 1853 by a Reverend Dr Reeves, who sold it for the same amount to the Church of Ireland Primate, Lord George Beresford. Beresford gave it to Trinity College in 1854. In addition to this there is a confirmatory *Life of Saint Patrick* by Muirehu, written in AD 699, a copy of which was discovered by scholars in Brussels.

Saint Patrick was a Roman Briton born between 385 and 390 AD, probably in the Roman city of Caerwent on the coast of South Wales, the burnt-out ruins of which lie ten miles from Newport. He was the son of a deacon and the grandson of a priest. He himself called the place of his birth 'Bannaven Taberniae', but scholars are yet to pinpoint either that or the place where he was captured by Irish raiders in a massive slave raid. This was in the year 406 AD, when Patrick was just sixteen years of age, and he was to spend the rest of his adolescence as a slave, tending flocks of sheep for his pagan master, Miliuce. During the six years of his captivity, he prayed literally night and day. Escaping to Britain around 412 AD, Patrick then trained as a priest in France, probably with Saint Germanus in Auxerre, and was very likely a monk at the Abbey of Lérins. After a dream in which

☐
Among Ireland's greatest benefactors are Mr and Mrs William Bowen Bourn of California, and their son-in-law, Mr Arthur Vincent, who presented Muckross House and its 10,000-acre estate to the Irish government for use as a national park. Muckross House (above left) is now a folk museum. Remaining pictures: simple but colourful Kerry shopfronts.

There are probably more pubs to the square mile in Kerry than in any other Irish county, and their regular customers (above, left and facing page top) are more likely to be Gaelic-speakers.

The first thing that strikes you about the pubs of Kerry (above and right) is that they resound with the accents of Gaelic-speakers – to some ears the softness of their accent is far superior to the lilt of the Corkman, the heavy accent of the Dubliner, or the metallic ring of a Belfast voice.

the Irish people begged him to return and convert them, he went back to the land of his former captivity in 432 AD as a bishop and spent some thirty years bringing Christianity to the Irish tribes. He founded his See at Armagh in 444 AD and died in Saul on 17th March, 461.

It says much for the character of the Saint, and that of the Celts themselves, that Patrick succeeded in converting the Irish without losing his life in the process. He overcame the sorcery of the Druids, matched the all-powerful bardic poets with his Christian mysticism, and had an enormous influence over the daughters of Irish kings, who flocked to embrace Christianity. Indeed, during his missionary life Patrick must have personally converted and baptised thousands of Irish pagan kings, queens, princes, princesses, Druids, bards, lawyers and warriors.

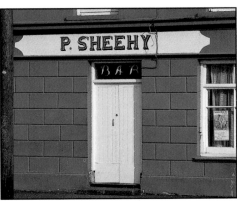

Sheehy (above left) is an historic name in Kerry. This clan originated in Scotland and came to Ireland in the twelfth century as bodyguards to royalty.

Left: misty sunshine falling on the Gap of Dunloe, a four-mile-long ravine near Killarney, and (below) neat fields of pasture on the Dingle Peninsula.

□

Above: the great conical bulk of Masatiompan looms out of the Atlantic Ocean at Brandon Head on the Dingle Peninsula.

Far left: a Kerryman smiles for the photographer and (below) the Slieve Miskish Mountains meet the sea. You can still hear the 'clack' of ungreased cart wheels (left) on the lanes of Kerry.

Paul Gallico, the American writer who loved Ireland and knew it so well, wrote a life of Saint Patrick while living in Ashford Castle in Cong, County Mayo, and called it quite simply *The Steadfast Man*. Saint Patrick was just that, possessing that British virtue, so lacking in the Celtic character, of tenacity of purpose. Certainly, having spent six years in captivity in Ireland, it is reasonable to assume that Patrick would have had a working knowledge of everyday, spoken Irish, a distinct asset in his later work, and from his years in Slemish he would also have gained a deep insight into the astute and volatile mind of the Celt.

Irish language, music and culture owes more to Indo-Eurasian than to Nordic or European culture, having taken its philosophy mainly from Greece. With its soil untrodden by the legions of Rome, Ireland remained totally Celtic and in no way Roman. To some extent, Irish people were

There are still many
traditional small farms
(this page) operating in
Kerry, smallholdings
whose owners 'foot' their
own turf for fuel and
keep small herds of cows
for milk.

Right: Black Valley and Cummeenduff Glen. Below: the lavishly decorated interior of Muckross House (facing page bottom), a

nineteenth-century mansion, and (bottom right) Muckross Abbey, a ruined Franciscan abbey of the fifteenth century, both south of Killarney.

Left: a shipwreck only yards from the beach at Coumeenoole, a small village at the foot of Mount Eagle near Slea Head.

☐
Below: the South Pole Inn in the village of Anascaul, where Thomas Crean, who took part in the Scott Expedition, was born. Right: Main Street, Dingle.

receptive of the message that Patrick brought them because they understood mysticism and also had an immense love of nature, having made gods of the elements of fire, earth, air and water. The Irish poetic mind was in sympathy with the story of the Galilean, the rebel Jew who had been publicly rejected as a king by Pontius Pilate, the Roman Governor who had turned Him over to his troops to be flogged, spat upon, slapped in the face, crowned with thorns and forced to carry His cross through the streets to be the centrepiece of a Roman crucifixion. They could imagine someone being nailed and exhibited naked before men on a tree, His side pierced by a Roman soldier's spear, His garments played for in a game of dice by members of the cohort who later guarded his tomb, and were blinded by the light of His resurrection.

These events were akin to the heroic sagas of the Ulster Mythological Cycle, akin – albeit with crucial differences – to the story of the death of Cú Chulainn, the Hound of Ulster, who was wounded and tied to a standing stone by the belt of his sword to die fighting against countless numbers of Queen Maeve of Connacht's warriors. This was the stuff of ancient Irish sagas, where it was thought better to live nobly for a day in freedom than to live a life of ignominy in slavery. This was the stuff of the Land of Tir-na-Og, the Land of Eternal Youth, the world of Life Everlasting – the world for which the Irish Celt most yearned.

At the crossroads of the path which led from the darkness of the Ireland of the pagan Druids with that leading to the light of this new Ireland of the Risen Christ stands the ancient Irish Saga of the story of *Oidhe Chloinne Lir, The Fate of the Children of Lir*. In this story it is related that Queen

' … If a sound arose, it was but what its own whispering waters made;
or the herdsboy's whistle faintly echoed from far-off fields and meadows;
or the hoarse and lonesome caw of the rook,
as he winged his heavy flight towards some fertile place.'

(John Banim)

☐ Facing page: Connor Pass, which crosses the Dingle Peninsula from Dingle to the bays of Brandon and Tralee. Carrantuohil (left), the highest mountain in Ireland, is set amid Macgillycuddy's Reeks. Below left: Cummeenduff Glen at the foot of Macgillycuddy's Reeks. Below: a Kerry standing stone.

☐ Left: a simple track leads to a lonely croft on the Dingle Peninsula.

Below left: loughs Gal and Clogharee, joined by a patch of
sunshine in the Brandon Mountains, and (bottom) loughs
Clogharee and Atlea form a foreground to Brandon Bay. Below
right: the long finger of Inch in Dingle Bay.

Aoifé, a warrior princess of the Land of Shadows and a jealous
stepmother, waved her magic wand and changed the fair child of King Lir,
Fionnghualia and her three brothers into four white swans. As such, they
were not to regain their human form again until the coming of the
Tailchenn to Ireland, the 'Shavenhead' (the name the bardic Druids gave
to Saint Patrick because of his strange form of tonsure), who would signal
their release by the sounding of his first Mass bell. At its tolling, the three
brothers were in terror, but their sister, Fionnghuala, recognised the 'bell
of the cleric' summoning them to return to human form to attend the
Banquet of the Body and Blood of Christ. Of this the ancient
bardic poet wrote:

Right: Connor Pass, which lies between the peaks of Ballsitteragh and Slievanea in the Brandon Mountains (bottom right) on the Dingle Peninsula (below). Bottom left: a burst of sunshine highlights a tapestry of Killarney fields.

'Listen to the Cleric's bell;
Lift your wings and soar upwards;
Give thanks to God for its coming
And be grateful for having heard it.

Fitting it is that ye be ruled by it;
It is the bell that shall liberate you from pain,
Shall bring you away from the rocks and stones
And from the furious currents.

I say to you, therefore,
Make ye a profession of proper faith,
Ye comely Children of Lir
Listen to the bell of the Cleric!

☐
Staigue Fort (facing page), which lies between Sneem and Waterville, is thought to be the finest example of a stone fort in Ireland. Its north wall rises to eighteen feet in height and is especially well preserved. Above: Muckross Abbey, a Franciscan friary which Cromwell's troops ransacked in the seventeenth century. Right: stooks of hay mimic the rock stacks on Coumeenoole Strand and (above right) a lonely Kerry ruin rises from the pasture.

☐ Right: the little village of Adare, once voted the prettiest village in the land, and (below) cows on the road to Lough Gur, south of Limerick.

☐ Industry and agriculture contrast in Limerick. Above: a bauxite smelter on Aughinish Island and (right) harvest.

Limerick city (above) originated as a Danish
settlement of raiding Norsemen in the ninth century.
Later it was ruled by the Normans and, for a short
period of time, by the native O'Brien clan.

☐
Right: haymaking in
Killaloe, thirsty work that
would surely call for an
evening in the bar
(above).

Saint Patrick's Bell and its shrine can be seen in the National Museum of Ireland. It is a rough, iron bell made from two thin, shaped sheets, like the bells to be found hanging around the necks of Swiss cattle or sheep today. With a handle at the top and the four sides covering the bell's tongue held by simple rivets, the whole has been dipped in bronze. It was used in public for the first time since Saint Patrick's era in 1932, at the solemn High Mass celebrated before one million people on the occasion of the International Eucharistic Congress in Dublin. Its dull clang was heard again – this time on international television – during the High Mass celebrated by His Holiness Pope John Paul II in Phoenix Park in Dublin on 29th September, 1979. The bell shrine that covers the old iron bell was made in Armagh to the order of Donal O'Loughlin, King of Ireland, around the year 1091. It is made of bronze, richly ornamented with silver-gilt open work castings and detailed with gold filigree and glass studs of great beauty.

An appreciation of the power of the orator and the use of the spoken word was unique to Indo-Eurasian Celtic civilisation. A mystic like Patrick was very readily received by the Celts because they were accustomed to poets. The *fili*, the all-powerful poets of pre-Christian Ireland, were a class of greatly respected literary intellectuals who kept alive the spoken traditions of myths and heroic sagas. Patrick and the kings and poets cooperated in drawing up the *Seanchas Mór*, the law book of the Celtic Irish nation:

'Now until the coming of Patrick, speech was not allowed in Ireland but to three; to a historian for the telling of tales; to a poet for praise and satire; to a lawyer for just judgment. But after the coming of Patrick all speech of these men is under the yoke of the men of the sacred language, that is the scriptures.'

The people of Clare (above) are famous in history for returning radical Daniel O'Connell, 'The Liberator', as their Member of Parliament from 1828-31. They repeated the performance when they elected equally radical Eamon de Valera as their Sinn Fein MP in 1917.

☐
Right: a road, so straight it appears almost Roman, near Lisseycassey in central Clare. Below: the dry stonescape known as the Burren, in the north of the county, contrasts with flooded fields.

Right: farming country in Glenconaum, near Kalladysert, and (below) a fifteenth-century graveyard in Caher Connell, west of Lisdoonvarna. Below right: brown-trout fishing in Inchiquin Lough, just north of Corofin. On the banks of this small lough stand the ruins of Inchquin Castle, which date from the middle of the fifteenth century.

Alongside the oral poetic tradition there grew up the most exquisite and expert craftmanship which centred upon the vessels to be used in the Mass. The National Museum of Ireland today houses one of the greatest collections of gold ornaments in Europe, together with the silver Ardagh and Derrynaflan chalices.

The Ardagh Chalice was found over one hundred years ago by a youth who was digging potatoes in a place called Reerasta Rath near Ardagh in County Limerick. The silver chalice dates from the eighth century. Around its lip are etched the names of the apostles. Its superb decorations are comprised of bronze, gold, glass and rock crystal; based on La Tène interlacing lines, they include cloisonné enamelling and the finest filigree work. The Derrynaflan Chalice, equally beautiful and dating from the ninth century, was found in a Tipperary bog in 1980 by a father and son using a metal detector.

These physical examples of works of early Patrician Christian art can still be seen, as can the books of Patrick's words on ancient Irish vellum. In addition to his *Confession* and *Letter* we also have, from the Book of Armagh, the *Lorica*, or *Breastplate of Saint Patrick*. Here Patrick 'surrounds' himself with Christ in an invocation to the Holy Trinity to protect him from Druidic witchcraft. Legend has it that this was the prayer he used during his first encounter with the Druids at Tara. Popularly known as *The Deer's Cry*, even a verse in translation (from the Irish by Kuno Meyer) carries considerable power:

Top: the magnificent falls on the River Cullenagh at Ennistymon.
Above left: Shannon Airport and Industrial Estate, and (above right) the cliffs of Kilkee at Moore Bay, their savagery typical of the Clare coast.

Left and top: the Cliffs of Moher. Lying two miles or so from Ennistymon and rising seven hundred feet above the Atlantic Ocean, these magnificent cliffs extend for five rugged miles. Such is the force of the wind here that small waterfalls are often blown back up the cliff face, and even splinters of rock from the cliff can be found in the pastures above. Above: fine brown trout, a typical catch in the rivers of Clare.

In the centre of the Burren stands dramatic Poulnabrone Dolmen (right). The word 'dolmen' comes from a Breton-Gaelic word for a stone table. Dating from over 2,000 years before the birth of Christ, these Neolithic stones are thought to mark the burial place of chiefs. Below: a blacksmith in Bunratty and (bottom) a winter's evening in Doolin Bay.

'Long, long ago, beyond the misty space
Of twice a thousand years,
In Erin old there dwelt a mighty race,
Taller than Roman spears;
Like oaks and towers they had a giant grace,
Were fleet as deers,
With wind and waves they made their 'biding place,
These western shepherd seers.'

(Thomas D'Arcy McGhee 1825-1868)

*'I arise today
Through the strength of Heaven:
Light of sun,
Radiance of moon,
Splendour of fire,
Speed of lightning,
Swiftness of wind,
Depth of sea,
Stability of earth,
Firmness of rock.'*

There is scarcely a year that passes without the bogs and lakes of Ireland yielding up mysterious finds and treasures which help to deepen our knowledge of this Golden Age in the land of saints and scholars. In December 1986, for example, a unique and exquisitely designed eighth-century book shrine was recovered from the bed of a lake in the Midlands

□
The limestone rock garden of the Burren (left) extends for some fifty square miles north of Lisdoonvarna. Beneath the Burren lies the longest cave in Ireland. Above left: a folk park at Bunratty, which portrays typical fishermen's cottages, a forge and craft works. Above: a windy day in the Corra Valley.

Above: as tired as his donkey at the end of the day, a Clare
farmhand brings home a cartload of hay.

☐

The locals 'footing' turf and carrying it away on the backs of donkeys (right and below) may appear charming. In reality, this fuel all too frequently produces smoke but no fire, and cutting it is back-breakingly hard work.

and put on display in the National Museum in Dublin. The shrine took the form of a box or casket in which a copy of the Gospels had been kept. Highly ornate and embossed with a cross, the shrine was thirteen-inches long, eleven-inches wide and four-and-a-half inches deep. The cross was of gilt bronze and the decorative motifs on the cover were akin to those found on the Tara Brooch and in the Book of Kells.

There are a variety of places connected with Saint Patrick that may still be visited today. The most famous is Tara of the Kings, the hill in Meath where he made his first converts. At the Rock of Cashel, the 'Irish Acropolis' in County Tipperary, you can see the ancient Celtic cross that marks the spot where Patrick converted the King of Munster. Atop Croagh Patrick, Patrick's holy mountain in County Mayo, you are on the spot, 2,500 feet above Clew Bay, where he fasted for forty days and forty nights and, it is said, wrested from God the privilege of judging the Irish people on the Last Day. Lough Derg, 'St Patrick's Purgatory', in County Donegal,

Left: a blacksmith at Bunratty Folk Park revives an ancient art at the forge. Below and bottom left: aerial views of the Cliffs of Moher. Though the tremendous height of these cliffs is best appreciated from sea level, such a treacherous coastline makes sailing close to the rocks foolish. Bottom: ivy softens the outlines of a ruined church near Caher Connell.

*'Royal and saintly Cashel! I would gaze
Upon the wreck of thy departed powers,
Not in the dewy light of matin hours,
Nor the meridian pomp of summer's blaze,
But at the close of dim autumnal days,
When the sun's parting glance, through slanting showers,
Sheds o'er thy rock-throned battlements and towers
Such awful gleams as brighten o'er Decay's …'*

(*Sir Aubrey de Vere 1788-1846*)

four miles north of Pettigo, is also associated with the National Apostle. Today it is a flourishing centre of pilgrimages where over 30,000 people a year fast, pray and do penance for three days and two nights, including an all-night vigil.

In addition, here are literally hundreds of less famous places throughout Ireland associated with Saint Patrick. County Meath and North Connacht featured largely in his travels, and it is certain he journeyed right across the middle of Ireland, did a circuit of the northern half of the country, and went down through Leinster to the Rock of Cashel. At the start of his mission he arrived at the coast of Wicklow, and then made his way by sea past Lambay Island to anchor off the Skerries, where he took on fresh spring water at what is now known as Saint Patrick's Island. While he was doing so the natives of the Skerries stole his goat, skinned, cooked and ate it, and as a result the people of the Skerries are still known as the 'Skin-the-Goats' today. Saint Patrick founded his first church at Saul in the old barn of his former master, Dichu. The church at Slane is his, while his

☐

Facing page: the Rock of Cashel. Above and above right: a field of ragwort leads the eye to the gentle slopes of Slieve Kimalta, which rises to nearly 2,300 feet near Knockfune, while (right) a rape field ripens near Clonmel. Clonmel is renowned as the birthplace of Laurence Sterne, eighteenth-century author of the comic classic *Tristram Shandy*. It is also famous as the place where Cromwell met his most severe opposition, during his seige of the town in 1650.

bishopric was founded at Armagh. Saint Doolagh's ancient church near Portmarnock is associated with Patrick, and he built a church at the ford of Kells. Derrypatrick too, four miles from the hill of Tara, is a Patrician church, and he founded churches at Lough Ennell and some in Westmeath and County Leitrim. The church of Kilmore near Drumsna is his, and also one at Elphin. It is said that he built five churches in the Sligo area and seven in the Boyne and Roscommon area. Four churches were set up in County Mayo in the area of Clew Bay, and at Kiloney near Drumcliffe. In County Donegal near Raphoe he founded the church of Donaghmore. From County Donegal Patrick progressed to County Derry and County Tyrone, building churches near Bushmills and the Giants' Causeway. He erected churches in counties Cavan and Monaghan, and established one at Kilcock and another at Kilcullen, both in County Kildare. His progress through counties Carlow and Kilkenny brought him

☐

Above: rolling pastures near Clonmel stretch as far as the Knockmealdown Mountains. Right: a view across Lough Derg to Clare and Galway.

☐
Left, below and bottom right: the Glen of Aherlow in the Galtee Mountains, south of Tipperary.

☐
Left: as the road starts to dry in the sunshine of a spring morning, there is leisure to settle down and read a newspaper.

Below: green pasture around Clonmel. Tipperary is Ireland's
largest inland county and renowned hunting country. It is
acknowledged as a superb breeding ground for fine horses and
racing greyhounds.

to Cashel in County Tipperary, and to the founding of the church of
Ardpatrick in County Limerick. He must have founded in the region of one
hundred places of worship and his monk followers founded many
hundreds more.

Corkmen and Kerrymen, apparently, never had the chance to shake hands
with Saint Patrick, but they proudly claim, somewhat slyly, that Saint
Ciaran had 'pressed the flesh' in Cork and Kerry, before the more famous
Saint's arrival. Corkmen, the 'Texans' of Ireland, coyly observe that they
were already Christians before Saint Patrick set foot in the country, and it
is also quite possible that the men of County Waterford could count
themselves alongside the men of Cork and Kerry in the claim that they
were pre-Patrician Christians.

For the monk followers of Saint Patrick, exile from Erin was self-imposed –
the famous German monk Walafridus Strabo (Wilfrid the Squinter) wrote:
'Going on pilgrimages to foreign parts has become, for Irish monks,
second nature'. It is difficult to make a head count of Irish missionaries to
the Continent but, during the earliest days of the 'wanderers', it is
estimated that about twenty-five Irish monks went to Scotland, fifty to
England, nearly one hundred to France, over one hundred to Germany
and twenty to Italy. Each monastic foundation in these countries sent out
hundreds more missionaries, so that from the beginning of the fifth
century to the end of the tenth their numbers could have been
counted in thousands.

□
The Rock of Cashel (left), the Acropolis of Ireland, dominates the countryside on a limestone outcrop above the plains of Tipperary. It was the seat of the kings of Munster from 370 AD to 1101. Below: the ruins of Hore Abbey, built near the Rock in the eleventh century.

□
Above left: hedges lead the eye to the Knockwealdown Mountains, southwest of Clonmel. Cahir Castle (left) was erected in 1142 by Conor O'Brien, Prince of Thomond. Elizabeth I's Earl of Essex took it in 1599 and it was surrendered to Cromwell in 1650.

'The splendour falls on castle walls
And snowy summits old in story;
The long light shakes across the lakes,
And the wild cataract leaps in glory.'

(Alfred, Lord Tennyson 1809-1892)

These spiritual invaders of the Europe of the Dark Ages frequently travelled in groups of twelve like the first apostles, and were often led by a learned monk, abbot or bishop. A noisy bunch, they were also an astonishing sight. Dressed in a coarse, white woollen over-tunic and sometimes the semblance of a cowl, they had no possessions except knowledge – no gold, no silver. Some may have appeared to be rough and ready, not to say uncouth. Yet their deep-seated piety was unmistakeable. Such was their obvious delight in voyaging across dangerous and sometimes unchartered waters and tramping across unknown wastelands that many were said to have been born under a wandering star. Their passion for travel was insatiable, but their call was a genuine vocation to higher things, to the leading of a more ascetic life. They were not all that far distant in time from the days of Christ and the primitive faith set out by Saint Paul.

□
County Waterford, on the southern coast of Ireland, offers a great diversity of scenery. Facing page: the Silvermine Mountains. Above: scree falls to a wind-rippled lough in the Comeragh Mountains and (right) moorland meets pastureland near Knocknanask in the Knockmealdown Mountains.

☐
Right: a view of the Comeragh Mountains, which span the centre of the county. The highest peak here rises to over 2,500 feet.

☐
Above: threshing over an oil drum in a Waterford farmyard and (right) filling a pipe in the cool of the evening outside a country farmhouse.

Below: the thin threads of two waterfalls grace the slopes of the
Comeragh Mountains.

They travelled on foot. Unlike any other men in holy orders – who
favoured the small tonsure on the crown of the head – the Irish monks
wore their hair in a fashion which was perculiar to the Druidic Celts.
Continentals were astonished by, and in awe of, these men with their
heads shaven right across from ear to ear, leaving unshorn, however, half
the crown towards the front of the head. They wore their hair long at the
back of the neck, their locks hanging down to their shoulders. Each wore
simple, hand-made sandals and carried a crude, wooden staff, a leather
gourd for water and a small wallet for food and writing materials. They
spoke with passion and eloquence, at first through interpreters until they
had mastered the language of the country in which they were preaching
and teaching. They must have looked like spiritual hippies!

Their primary targets were the pagan tribes that had overrun Europe after
the fall of the Roman Empire. Rome finally fell to the German Visigoths,
led by Aleric, in 408. After them had come the cavalry of the Huns, led by
Attila, together with Gothic infantry – in all a horde of a million or so
barbarians without a written language or a rule of law between them. And
after them had come the Moslems who followed the teachings of
Muhammad Mahomet. Their progress west had only been halted by the
Franks in 732, under the command of Charles Martel, at Poitiers. Not all
that many years later Charlemagne held back the barbaric hordes from
the forests beyond the Rhine, and prevented the Saracens from
taking Provence.

◻ Vast supermarkets are not the norm in rural Ireland. The local shop (right) still survives. Sometimes it sells everything – rosaries around the cheese, draught Guinness, statues of the Sacred Heart. Below: traditional milk delivery.

The 'counter-invasion' of Irish monks was to lead to the gradual cultivation of the intellectual wasteland that was Europe after the invasions of the Dark Ages. Universities and other centres of learning in Europe established by these men were based on the monasteries at Armagh, Bangor, Clonamacnoise and Durrow from which they came. The 'wanderers' swept through Wales, Scotland and England and on to France, Belgium, Switzerland and Italy, reaching as far as the Danube and even the Volga. There was no stopping their progess – they travelled as far as Greenland and Iceland in the north and as far to the east as Jerusalem and even to Kiev.

In France their main base was established at Luxeuil. Charlemagne, who had witnessed them setting up their stalls in the markets and shouting 'No visible goods, knowledge for sale!', invited them to reform religion and education throughout his empire. Irish monasteries sprang from the famous monastery of Saint Gall in Switzerland. Saint Kilian evangelised

Above: the colours of a Waterford shop front are mimicked in the
make-up of this young clown.

☐
They have been making glass (this page) in Waterford since Elizabethan times, the first furnace being established near Dungarvan.
In the late 1950s, Waterford lead crystal became famous again. Now a highly skilled workforce of thousands produces Waterford glass for export all over the world.

France and Thuringia. Irish monks founded monasteries at Strasburg and at Friesing, Virgil became the Bishop of Salzburg, Saint Colman, became the martyr apostle of southern Austria and Saint Frindolin became the very first Bishop of Alsace. Marianus Scotus founded the monastery at Ratisbon, from which twelve other monasteries were born.
All were Irishmen.

The Irish tide soon swept over the Alps. In the middle of the sixth century, Saint Ursus was at work in Val d'Aosta and Saint Freidan was Bishop of Lucca. In the seventh century, mighty Saint Columbanus founded the famous monastery at Bobbio. Saint Cataladus of Lismore, County Waterford, was cast up by the sea on the coast at Taranto in a violent storm, ultimately to become the Bishop of Taranto. In the ninth century, Saint Donatus was made the Bishop of Fiesole.

The great monasteries brought about a cultural revolution in Europe, and the Continent was once again drawn into the production of classical and liturgical manuscripts and studies of all kinds in the spiritual life. During the Irish Golden Age, students at monastic universities sometimes numbered up to three thousand. From these mission stations they carried Christianity to every corner of pagan Europe, being in the full flower of missionary activity until the year 1000 or so. To them is owed the rebirth of Christianity in Western Europe. It is held by some that one of the secretaries to the great Saint Thomas Aquinas was an Irish monk from Cork. Certainly a man known as Peter the Irishman was an early professor of Saint Thomas at Naples. He taught the 'Dumb Ox of Sicily', 'whose

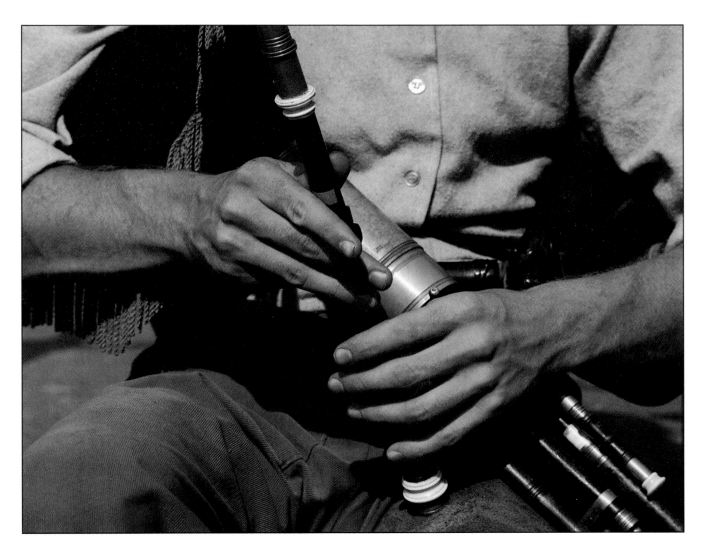

When Elizabeth I ordered the burning of all Irish war pipes, the
Irish took to making the more secretive vileann pipes (above),
which are played seated, the bellows worked by the arms –
'villeann' was the eighteeth-century Irish word for 'elbow'.

Wild, heather-covered slopes in the Monayullagh
Mountains (left) contrast with the classical severity of
the Bishop's Palace (top). Above: a cove near
Tramore, otherwise known as 'The Big Strand' – a town
famous for its horse races and its three sandy beaches.
The town lies eight miles south of Waterford City.

lowing would soon be heard all over the world', to read Aristotle in the original Greek, setting the angelic Doctor on his special path to becoming one of the greatest doctors in the history of the Church, renowned for his *Summa Theologica*.

The wandering monks were a disturbing lot sometimes. Many were abbots or bishops and local episcopal authority did not always welcome their using their episcopal powers in the course of their wanderings. Then, also, the Irish monks celebrated Easter at a different time from everyone else. They followed the old Paschal cycle, the same one Saint Patrick followed when he lit the first Paschal fire in Ireland on the Hill of Slane in County Meath, causing the High King of Tara to send for him for breaking the sacred annual black-out of the pagan Druids. And the strange tonsure of the Irish monks was ever a problem. For sure, the world did not always

□ Facing page: (top) Knocknanask and (bottom) the River Tar Valley in north Waterford. Below: a hill farm in the Drum Hills, south of Dungarvan. Curraghmore House (left) is the elegant seat of the Marquis of Waterford, set in a demesne of valleys and woods watered by the River Suir. The Round Tower (bottom) on the Bay of Ardmore dates from the ninth century.

This page: Irish craftsmen and women at work in the forge and at the spinning wheel, continuing a tradition of metalwork and weaving that is centuries old.

appreciate the work of these men at the time, but with hindsight, European civilisation has learned to understand their major contribution to restoring Christianity to the Continent of the Dark Ages.

In their Greek learning tradition the early Irish monks were very much aware that Saint Denis had declared that monks derived their very name from the Greek word monos, meaning 'alone', or 'unique' because of their attempts to lead lives of undivided unity with God. In trying to do so, they turned the spiritual world upside-down for, unlike the monks of other nations who lived and died in their monasteries, Irish monks figuratively took their monasteries with them on their spiritual wanderings. Morever, Irish monks were unique in that they did not enforce their nationality on

Top: an inquisitive collie puppy watches over a potato harvest.
Above left: ripe corn on Tory Hill, near Mullinavat and (above right) Inistioge, on the banks of the River Nore.

The cathedral city of Kilkenny (left) stands on the banks of the River Nore and is a very Norman town, possessing not only a cathedral but a medieval castle as well. The cathedral, which was built on the site where St Canice established his sixth-century monastery, was virtually destroyed by Cromwell and has been much restored. Below: Kilkenny farmland.

Graiguenamanagh (above), which means 'The Village of the Monks', is a splendidly situated village that lies on a bend in the River Barrow. The Cistercian Abbey of Duiske was founded there in the thirteenth century by William le Mareschal, Earl of Pembroke.

Above: Hook Head, a long, narrow peninsula known for its beautiful limestone corals, and (right) cliffs near Fethard, a Wexford town that dates back to medieval times.

others, but rather emptied themselves of this legacy and became citizens of the land in which they preached. But then the record of the Celts in receiving the message of Christ from Saint Patrick was also unique, in as much as the pagan Irish never martyred a missionary sent among them. As natural orators who loved truth, Irish missionaries were unusually good preachers and teachers, fortunate too in preaching the Gospel from a soundly united Christian base. Unlike their kind today, they were not obliged to suffer either a divided Christendom in Europe, or the horror of a native land where men and women destroy each other in the name of a religious bigotry based on hate.

□

Above: Dunbrody Abbey, built by the Normans in the twelfth century and once very important, and (above right) Hook Head Lighthouse standing sentinel over Doornoge Bay. Kilmore Quay (right), some thirteen miles from Rosslane, is a little-known seaside resort, but a well known deep-sea angling centre. A fantastic bird sanctuary on the Saltee Islands may be visited from the village.

Above: a poodle takes the air in the arms of its owner. Facing page top: the Ninety-Eight Memorial at New Ross. Facing page bottom: (right) a Wexford man and (left) his pony and trap – one of the finest ways to see the Wexford countryside.

The whole epic story of the Irish *peregrini* might well be summed up by
the Irish poet, Arthur O'Shaughnessy, who wrote:

'We are the music-makers,
And we are dreamers of dreams,
Wandering by lone sea-breakers,
And sitting by desolate streams,
World-losers and world-forsakers,
On whom the pale moon gleams:
Yet we are movers and shakers
Of the world forever, it seems.'

□
Lady's Island (left), the site of an ancient Augustinian monastery, is a place of annual pilgrimage. It lies in Lady's Island Lake in an inlet near Carsore Point. Below left: the J. F. Kennedy Memorial Park near Aughclare. Wexford is forever associated with this president, whose great-grandfather was born in a cottage at Dunganstown nearby. Below: the mighty River Slaney, which empties into Wexford Harbour.

Few would argue over the meaning of the word 'scholar', accepting that it means a learned person, especially one who is versed in the classics of ancient Greece and Rome. The definition of a saint, however, is more difficult, but few would quarrel with the view of the distinguished Engish Jesuit scholar, Father C. C. Martindale:

'Saints are, anyway, real and historical persons, who survive not just as memories, but as forces, and do so, because they had something special in them – were not just men of flamboyant vision like Cecil Rhodes, or of sweeping unscrupulous genius like Napoleon, nor just Quixotes, let alone folk of personal charm or beauty – more Helens of Troy, an up-to-date Adonis. The speciality that was theirs can be shown to be, in all cases, an intense belief in God, an intense love of Jesus Christ and intense devotion for Their sakes to the service of mankind (albeit in the most widely divergent ways – but still, always the service and salvation of their fellow human for Christ's sake).'

Left: Dunbrody Abbey in spring. Below: Johnstown Castle, a beautiful mansion that incorporates the tower of a thirteenth-century fortress. Now an agricultural college, the castle also houses a rural history museum.

☐
Carlow (left and facing page) is the smallest county in Ireland. Most of it is fertile farmland through which flows the River Slaney. The ruins of Ballymoon Castle (above), one of the earliest Norman strongholds built in Ireland, lie near Muine Bheag.

While this definition is very precise and clear, there are other definitions equally applicable to the early Irish saints. Carl Gustav Jung, an internationally acclaimed Christian psychologist, maintains that:

'Saints are those people who had attained unity and wholeness in their own personality, and they are the flowers, the fruits, and the seeds produced by the tree of humanity, and as such they became models for all of us; they are true sons of God, and the memory of them never withers and fades.'

Though of some of these early Irish saints little is known, of others a very great deal can be discovered from contempory sources. For many, the medieval hagiographers 'gilded the lily' in their over-enthusiasm, a zeal that was a product of the the age of chivalry and romance in which they lived. In other cases the Celtic Church has the advantage of on-the-spot reporting, much of which is surprising in its detail, when recounting the lives of saints. Alongside this is a reliance on the basic facts about the saints as told by poets, harpists and shanachies (story tellers).

'Two thousand years 'mid sun and storm,
That tall tower has lifted its mystic form.
The yew-tree shadowing the aisle,
'Twixt airy arch and mouldering pile,
And nigh the hamlet that chapel fair
Shew religion has dwelt, and is dwelling there.'

(Thomas Davis 1814-1845)

The cult of martyrs, and the communion of saints as observed in the early Celtic Church followed the guidelines set down by the great Saint Augustine in his great work *The City of God*:

'We build temples to our martyrs not like temples for the gods, but as tombs for mortal men, whose spirits live with God. We do not build altars on which to offer sacrifice to martyrs, but we offer sacrifice to God alone, who is both ours and theirs. During this sacrifice they are named in their place and order, in so far as they are men of God who have overcome the world by confessing God, but they are not invoked by the priest who offers sacrifice. He offers sacrifice to God, not to them (although it is celebrated in their memory) because it is God's priest, not the priest of the martyrs. The sacrifice is the body of Christ.'

☐
County Wicklow, lying south of Dublin, is the 'Garden of Ireland', having undulating park land, small granite mountains and hosts of lakes, rivers and waterfalls. Above: bogland near Lough Dan in the Wicklow Mountains and (right) falls on the Glenmacnass River, near Laragh. Above right: an old iron gate frames a distant peak near Enniskerry.

In writing the history of the lives of the saints, 'mortal men, whose spirits live with God', as Saint Augustine called them, there is a need not only to avoid the excesses of piety evident in the embellishments of medieval writers, but also the enthusiastic nonsense offered by many Irish national revivalist writers of the Victorian era. In all good faith and full of their new-found vision of Romantic Ireland, but often without a reasonably balanced and researched scholarship, they 'painted' pictures of a land of sun-flecked mountains, Irish wolfhounds, round towers and warriors 'taller than Roman spears'. This school of 'shamrockery' historians saw Ireland's history through green-tinted spectacles. To them, the Ireland of this time was simply a land of bearded chieftains, elegant princesses, wise bards, harpists, illuminators of manuscripts, chess-masters, and nuns and monks clinging to the seaweed of their anchorite, beehive dwellings, all Irish speaking, occasionally breaking into classical Greek or Latin, and with a flow of *bon mots* and epigrams which would have done credit to Oscar Wilde or James Joyce. These were the foundations of the spiritual invaders of Europe, according to the Victorian Gaels.

This over-romantic view of Irish history should definitely be avoided. 'History', it has been said, 'is a lie agreed upon'. 'History is more or less bunk' said Henry Ford, the Irishman who left his cabbage patch in County Cork to take the emigrant ship to America, and 'History is written by the victors' said the Irish scholar and historian, Cardinal Tomas O'Fiaich, 113th successor to Saint Patrick in the See of Armagh. Bearing these definitions in mind, and regarding the word in the true sense of its Greek

Sally Gap (above), from the Irish for 'Saddle Gap', lies over 1,600 feet up in the heart of the Wicklow Mountains, near the source of the River Liffey – a remote, romantic and wild spot.

☐
Below: a stream graced with gorse near Hollywood in the Wicklow Mountains and (right) the start of the Inchavore River. Bottom: a Wicklow stone circle.

origin – historia, meaning 'inquiry' – a narrative of the history of this Ireland of saints and scholars must stay with the known facts given by contemporary observers, rejecting medieval embellishments and Victorian values.

While, particularly during the sixth century, Irish monks were spreading through Europe, scholars from Europe crossed to Ireland to study at the monastic universities. After all, it took only three or four days and nights to sail from the valley of the Loire to the mouth of the River Lee in County Cork, and thence to the monastic university of Bangor in County Down.

The Venerable Bede, the English historian, paid tribute to the generosity of the Irish monks of this time when he wrote:

The Piper Stones (above) at Athgreany are a circle of thirteen prehistoric
granite stones. Their name derives from the tradition that fairy bagpipers
played in this secluded spot. Facing page: Sugarloaf Mountain, which
attains 1,600 feet in height near Kilmacanoge.

'The sun, with wondrous excess of light,
Shone down and glanced
Over seas of corn
And lustrous gardens aleft and right.
Even in the clime
Of resplendent Spain,
Beams no such sun upon such a land ...'

(James Clarence Mangan 1803-1849)

'Many of the nobles of the English nation and lesser men also had set out hither (to Ireland, for the love of God and the love of learning), forsaking their native island either for the grace of sacred learning or a more austere life. And some of them, indeed, dedicated themselves faithfully to the monastic life, while others rejoiced rather to give themselves to learning, going about from one master's cell to another. All these the Irish willingly received, and saw to it to supply them with food and drink by day, without charge, and books for their studies, and teaching, free of charge.'

Of the many hundreds of monks heading into Europe, Saint Columbanus had arguably the greatest influence on the restoration of Christain scholarship, learning and piety there, as his monk followers founded well

over one hundred monasteries which remained 'intellectual fortresses' right into the Middle Ages. The austere rule of Columbanus lasted through the initial clay-and-wattle days of the first Christian churches, and his work is, in our time, largely underestimated or overlooked because, as the scholar Cardinal Tomas O'Fiach has pointed out, 'History is written by the victors' and in the case of Columbanus the 'victors' were the followers of the more gentle rule of the great Saint Benedict. Saint Benedict took over where the more austere rule of Saint Columbanus left off, and clay-and-wattle chapels and monasteries gave way to the permanent stone buildings of monk-masons, particularly the Normans.

Left: Bray Promenade. Bray is a seaside resort which lies thirteen miles south of Dublin city. The 'gateway' to County Wicklow, it has a beach and an esplanade over a mile in length. Below left: sheep safely grazing in fields near Tinahely in the Derry River valley and (below) beautiful Glendalough, the most picturesque glen in Wicklow.

So far in this narrative we have mentioned Saint Gall of Switzerland, Kilian of Franconia, Virgil of Salzburg, Colman of Austria, Marianus Scotus of Ratisbon, Ursus of Val d'Aosta, Freidan of Lucca, Columbanus of Bobbio, Cataldus of Taranto, and Donatus of Fiesole. Of these apostles, Columbanus was the towering spiritual colossus, yet to this illustrious number must be added one of the loveliest of men ever to have come out of Ireland, Saint Colmcille. Also known as Columba of Iona (521-597), the life of this Donegal prince, Irish poet, great Gael, prophet extraordinary, Apostle of Scotland and 'Dove of the Church' is as well documented as that of most men in history. He was referred to by the Venerable Bede, and his companions, Cuimine and Adamnan, abbots of Iona, wrote his biography.

First of all, Colmcille was a builder of monasteries in Ireland itself. Then he became famous abroad, and was more popularly known under the title of Saint Columba, Abbot of Iona, for his mission to Scotland. He was born at Gartan in the northwest of Donegal, a county of unsurpassable

Bray Head (above), near Bray (top), rises nearly 800 feet above sea level
and affords the climber magnificent, panoramic views of Dublin Bay.
South of the head stands the old-fashioned fishing village of Greystones,
while adjacent lies the Glen of Dargle River, thick with woods.

'I see his blood upon the rose
And in the stars the glory of his eyes,
His body gleams amid eternal snows,
His tears fall from the skies.'

(Joseph Mary Plunkett 1877-1916)

Facing page: watery sunshine over Lough Tay in the Wicklow Mountains. Glencree Valley (below) leads to Glencree, one of the prettiest villages in Ireland.

loveliness that boasts a rugged Atlantic coastline and deep blue lakes set amid majestic rocky mountains and tree-lined valleys. Northwest of Gartan stands the shining white mountain of Errigal, the Fujiyama of Ireland. Adjacent to Gartan today lies fabulous Glenveagh Park, a haunt of red deer, peregrines, merlins and eagles that embraces magnificent Lough Veagh. Colmcille's birthplace was and is a place of awesome beauty.

Every time I have visited it I am conscious of seeing in the distance the white horse of Colmcille. But that is quite another story. Still standing on the route from Gartan to Derry is the Grianan of Aileach, the Stone Palace of the Sun, which was built 1,700 years before Christ. In Colmcille's time this vast stone fortress atop the Hill of Grianan was the residence of the O'Neills, the kings of Aileach. The Ui Neill were descendants of Niall of the Nine Hostages, High King of Ireland in the fifth century. Colmcille came from this noble lineage. Within Glenveagh National Park there is a flagstone on the hillside west of the lake at Lacknacoo which is said to mark the spot where Colmcille was born. Dermot Walsh, the proprietor of the Carrigart Hotel in Carrigart, would have me believe that the two small cup marks on the flattened stone surface on the roadside at Gartan are the knee-prints of Colmcille and I am quite prepared to believe him! Half a mile north are the remains of a chapel dedicated to the Saint which was built in 1622.

Colmcille was born on 7 December, 521. Feidhlimidh, his father, was a grandson of Conall Gulban of the very noble lineage of Niall of the Nine Hostages, the greatest royal King in Irish history. On his mother's side he

Connolly's Folly (left) was built in 1740 in the grounds of Carton House, a splendid eighteenth-century mansion designed by Richard Cassels that lies at Maynooth.

Above: a grey and a skewbald graze companionably in the Kildare countryside. Traditional Irish music is played on a diversity of instruments, from the old 'squeeze-box' (right) and the penny whistle to the elegant Irish harp and flute. Facing page: a detail from Moone High Cross in the demesne of Moone Abbey House, Moone.

was related to Cathair Mor and the heroic kings of Leinster. Most of his cousins were royal kings during his lifetime, and he too could have been a king, possibly the Ard-Ri, the High King of Ireland, had he chosen this course. Instead, he studied as a monk, first under a local priest, Cronaghan, and then under the spiritual guidance of Saint Finnian, Abbot of Clonard, in the monastery at Moville, where he received minor orders and was ordained a priest. Clonard in County Meath is today a tiny village off the main Dublin-to-Mullingar road, about nine miles from Kinnegad. There are no signs at all today that in the sixth century this was a great monastic university which attracted literally thousands of students from all over Ireland, England and the Continent.

Colmcille became a monk member of the community of his school chum, Saint Mobhi, at Glasnevin and then founded his first monastery in Derry in

'Good are they at man-slaying feats,
Melodies over meats and ale,
Of woven verse they wield the spell,
At chess-craft they excel the Gael.'

(From the 12th century 'Book of Leinster',
translated by Professor Kuno Meyer 1858-1919)

546. The monastery he built was on land given to him by his royal relatives, a couple of miles from the awe-inspiring Grianan of Aileach. Here he found great peace in its 'crowds of white angels'. While all physical traces of monasticism in Clonard have disappeared, its people kept the faith down through the ages. Cardinal Glennon, Archbishop of St. Louis, Missouri, was born there in 1862.

Ten years after the establishment of the monastery at Derry, in 556, Durrow Monastery was built in County Offaly, the very centre of Ireland. In the seventh century, the famous Book of Durrow was written here, and can be seen today in the Trinity College Library in Dublin. The land for this monastery was given to Saint Colmcille by Aedh, son of Brendan, a

Facing page: a Kildare cottage window. Religion plays a crucial part in Irish rural life. Right: Castletown House, near Celbridge, a superb Georgian mansion now owned by the Irish Georgian Society, and (below) Kildare pasture, typical of a county renowned for its breeding of fine thoroughbred horses.

local prince. The only surviving relic of the old monastery is a tenth-century Celtic high cross. It is a truly magnificent piece of Celtic stone carving, depicting on its east face the sacrifice of Isaac and Christ in his glory, the harpist King David on his left and David killing a lion on his right. On the west side soldiers guard the tomb of Christ, and the scourging of Christ at the pillar, the arrest of Christ and his Crucifixion are depicted. Adam and Eve, and Cain slaying Abel are portrayed on the south face, while on the north side the Holy Family flies into Egypt.

Then the great monastery at Kells was founded in the northwest of County Meath at Ceanannus Mór, as it is called today – the 'Great Residence'. Kells really came into its own when the monks from Iona, on the run from the raiding Vikings, sought refuge there in the ninth century. Here we still have Saint Colmcille's House, typically high roofed, like Saint

Kevin's Church in Glendalough in County Wicklow and Cormac's Chapel in Cashel in County Tipperary. A round tower, one hundred feet in height, still stands, as does a beautiful and ornate South Cross dedicated to Saint Patrick and Saint Colmcille. The world fame of the monastery of Kells lies in the fact that the Book of Kells, an illuminated manuscript of the four Gospels in Latin, was produced here. It is considered to be the finest example of Celtic illumination and, like the Book of Durrow, is on show in Dublin's Trinity College.

Churches were founded in County Dublin, at Drumcliff in County Sligo, and on the remote Tory Island off the north coast of County Donegal either by Saint Colmcille in person or by his followers. Some scribes would have us believe that Colmcille and his disciples founded one hundred churches in Ireland. In 563, perhaps rather abruptly, the Saint set

☐
Facing page: a grisly trio of desiccated bodies in the crypt of St Michan's Church, Dublin, whose preservation is made possible by the very dry atmosphere in this limestone building. Right and below: St Patrick's Cathedral, built on a site where the saint was said to have baptised converts.

☐
Dublin is a city of no less than three cathedrals: the Cathedral of St Mary in Marlborough Street, built between 1815 and 1825, Christ Church Cathedral (above), financed by Strongbow between 1172 and 1222 and now Church of Ireland, and St Patrick's Cathedral, founded in 1190.

Above: the altar of St Patrick's Cathedral, and (facing page) the
tombs of Strongbow and his son in Christ Church Cathedral.

off with his companions for Scotland, bound for the tiny Isle of Iona, in those days part of the Kingdom of Dal Riada, settled and run by Irishmen. In due course, these men of Iona not only converted Scotland, but also opened a door on Europe.

The reason for Colmcille's departure could have been a very simple one – a desire to go into voluntary exile for the sake of Christ. However, the more likely, and more romantic, reason has its roots in the very origins of the law of copyright, the exclusive right of an author to his original work. This version of Colmcille's exile sees it as an attempt by the Saint to atone for his responsibility for a battle between his monastery and a high king. The roots of the dispute between the two of them lay in the fact that Colmcille made a copy of a psalter belonging to Saint Finian of Moville. Saint Finian claimed the copyright, and Saint Colmcille refused to part with his copy. The High King, Diarmuid, was asked to give a ruling and

'Shore of fine fruit-bended trees,
Shore of green grass-covered leas;
Old plain of Ir, soft, showery,
Wheatful, fruitful, fair, flow'ry.

Home of priest and gallant knight
Isle of gold-haired maidens bright
Banba of the clear blue wave
Of bold hearts and heroes brave.'

(Translator unknown)

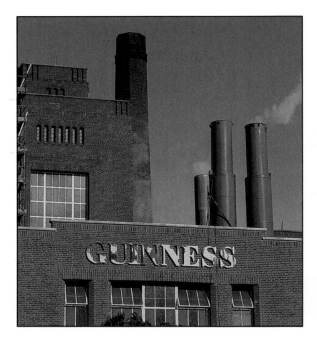

This page: the famous Guinness Brewery, one of the sights of Dublin, and (facing page) satisfaction as a Guinness drinker finishes a pint.

declared, 'to every cow its calf, and to every book its copy'. As Colmcille was of royal blood, he was able to call upon the support of his many princely cousins and defeat the King, with a heavy loss of life – three thousand men were said to have been slain – , in the Battle of Cul Dreimhne in 561. It is widely held that Colmcille repented this bloodshed and went into exile as a penance. Where his Monastery of Drumcliff once stood there still stands, by the roadside, a beautifully sculptured Celtic cross. There also stands the stump of a round tower, and across the road in front of the old Protestant church is the grave of the poet W.B. Yeats, with its stark message:

'Cast a cold eye
On life, on death.
Horseman pass by!'

At Cul Dreimhne itself, the scene of this 'Battle of the Books' near
Drumcliff, the atmosphere is charged with history. The whole battlefield is
dominated by the brooding, bare Benbulben, the Table Mountain of
Ireland, and is itself the reputed deathplace of the Celtic pre-Christain
hero, Diarmuid. Standing on the plain of Cul Dreimhne on a mist-
enshrouded morning, you can almost see helmeted and leather-cloaked
armed men advancing on the plain, and hear the neighing of horses, the
clash of arms and the cries of the warriors of Erin.

☐
Left: canoeists paddle past Dublin's Georgian Canal Hotel. Below: the Parnell Monument on O'Connell Street.

☐
There are some Dubliners who still regret that they cannot anymore buy a half a pound of rashers when they go to buy stamps in the General Post Office (above and facing page bottom right) in Dublin's O'Connell Street.

Headquarters of the Irish Volunteers during the 1916 Easter Rising, it was here, in this rather splendid building, that the Republic of Ireland was proclaimed. Left: the capital's Saturday shoppers.

Whether the battle of Cul Dreimhne took place or not, Colmcille's
biographer, Adamnan, is certain that the Saint left Ireland for Scotland
'wishing to be an exile for Christ', while the Venerable Bede is quite
adamant that he left Ireland 'in order to preach'. Either way, for the
remainder of his days, Colmcille lived in voluntary exile on the tiny,
windswept and barren island of Iona, returning to Ireland only on very
rare but important occasions. He was in a deep trauma at the thought of
exile from Erin, and his royal kinsmen in beautiful Donegal. It was
summed up in his own words, thus:

□
Top: the saddlery department of Brown Thomas
Department Store in Grafton Street. Above: Halfpenny
Bridge, Dublin's prettiest footbridge.

Below and bottom: Queen Maev Bridge and (right) Halfpenny Bridge at twilight, when the river view seems almost Parisian. The Liffey, the Anna Livia of James Joyce, was once much used by Guinness barges taking barrels of the black brew from the brewery to waiting vessels at the mouth of the estuary. The classic cry to skippers lowering their funnels under the bridges was 'Bring us back a parrot!'

'There is a grey eye
That looks upon Erin;
It shall not see during life
The men of Erin or their wives.
My vision o'er the brine I stretch
From the ample oaken boards,
Large is the tear of my soft grey eye
When I look back upon Erin'.

The life of the monks of Iona was one of obedience, prayer, fasting, celibacy, hospitality, humility, kindness to animals and moderation in all things. The pagan Picts of Scotland were the first evangelical target, so Colmcille and a few companions headed for Loch Ness and the idol-worshipping king at Iverness, King Brude, whom he converted. The Highlands, the Lowlands and the Scottish Islands, the Orkneys, the Shetlands, the Faroes and the Hebrides, all fell to the wisdom of this tall, powerful and strikingly handsome poet-prince priest. His personal

☐

There are still many traditional eighteenth-century and nineteenth-century shops (left and facing page) remaining in Dublin, and the service in them is as unhurried and as courteous as it has always been.

The back streets (above) of Dublin are seldom seen by the visitor, but they are deserving of more attention, especially as they are in danger of being destroyed by developers.

magnetism even effected a typically Irish compromise over the position of the Irish in Scotland, which was in dispute. It was agreed, under Colmcille's guidance, that the Irish high kings would supply a fleet for defence purposes while the Scots supplied the army.

Some years before his death, the sheer physical strain of missionary travel overtook Colmcille, and he spent the latter years of his life transcribing books and composing poetry. The poem *Altus Prosator*, an Irish *Dies Irae* is probably his, as are likely to be two other moving poems in Latin, *In Te Christe* and *Noli Pater*. His work as a scribe can be seen in the *Cathach of Colmcille* in the Royal Irish Academy in Dublin. The *Cathach* was enshrined in silver and wood, venerated in chuches and used in battle by his Donegal O'Donnell kinsmen. His biographer, Adamnan, wrote of him:

'He was angelic of aspect, clean in speech, holy in deed, of pleasant disposition, great in counsel. He could not pass ever a single hour without applying himself either to prayer or reading or writing or to some manual labour. By day and by night he was so occupied in unwearied exercises of fasts and vigils that the burden of any one of these special labours might be beyond human endurance. And amid all this he was beloved by all, ever showing a happy, holy countenance and gladdened in his innermost heart by the joy of the Holy Spirit.'

Above: outside a Dublin bar. The bar-tenders of Dublin pubs are known as 'Grocer's Curates', perhaps because of the skill and reverence they demonstrate in drawing a pint, and topping it with its pure white collar. The majority are not Dubliners, but are the sons of farmers from the country. They are courteous, well informed and well read.

Above: cigarettes all round in a Dublin back street. Left: 'The Long Hall', a fine old Dublin bar. In the older pubs of the capital, the enclosed 'snug', for privacy, has all the air of a confessional.

□
In what is left of Georgian Dublin, in places such as Merrion Square (bottom), the classic doorways (remaining pictures) have been lovingly preserved.

Adamnan writes very simply of his death:

'He and his dutiful attendant Diarmuid go to bless the granary which was nearby. When the Saint had blessed it and two heaps of corn stored up in it, he uttered these words, "Greatly do I congratulate the monks of my household that this year, also, if I should perchance have to depart from you, you will have enough for the year without stint. In the sacred volumes this day is called the Sabbath which is interpreted, Rest. And this day is truly a Sabbath day for me."

And while the Saint, weary with age, rested, behold his white horse, his faithful servant, runs to him, the one that used to carry the milk pails to and fro between the byre and the monastery. And coming up to the Saint

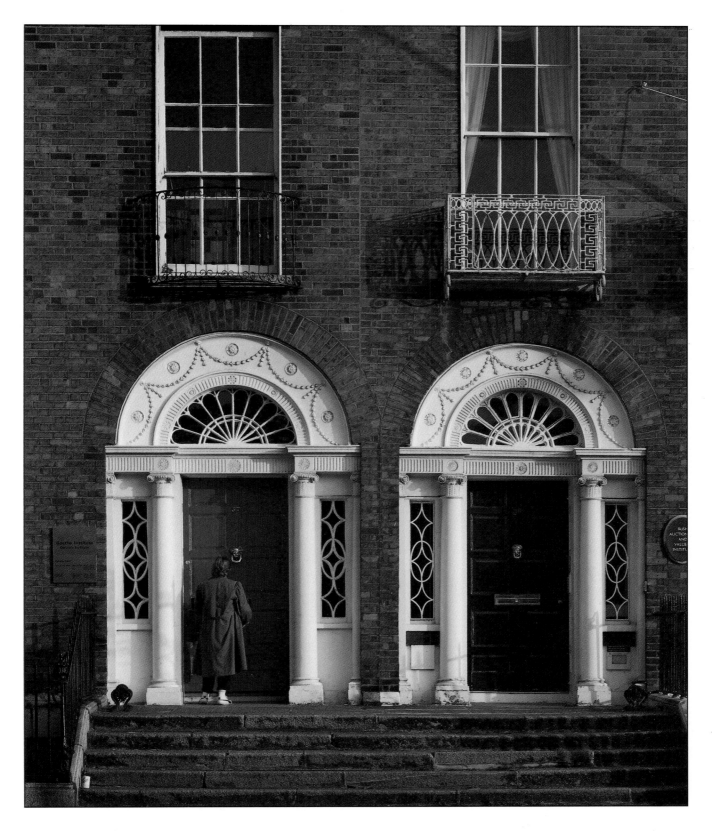

he lays his head upon his breast, knowing that his master was soon to leave him.

Returning to the monastery, he [Colmcille] sat in his cell transcribing the psalter and coming to that verse in the thirty-third psalm where it is written. "But they that seek the Lord shall not want any good thing", he says "Here I must stop at the foot of this page, let Baoithin write what follows."

When the bell began to toll at midnight he goes to the church and falls down in prayer at the altar. Diarmuid then lifts up the holy right hand of the Saint that he may bless the choir of monks. And after signifying his holy benediction, he immediately breathed forth his spirit.'

Thus Saint Colmcille died at the age of seventy-six on the Sabbath, 9th June, 597. His missionaries went on to conquer Northumbria, the Isle of Man and southern England for the Christian faith.

Saint Columbanus was born in the western part of the bountiful Province of Leinster, and like Saint Colmcille, was also a nobleman. Educated by Saint Sinell at the monastic university of Cleenish in County Fermanagh, Columbanus went on to higher studies under the tutelage of Saint Comgall at the famous monastic university of Bangor in County Down. Saint Comgall, who died around 600, had been a soldier before he became a monk and had in turn been taught by Saint Finian of Clonard and Saint Ciaran of Clonmacnoise. Bangor University, which he founded, was famous throughout Europe, attended by thousands of students from all over the Continent.

Around the year 590, Saint Columbanus set sail for the Continent with twelve monks from Bangor. He had no fixed plan and certainly no fixed abode in mind, and sought only to go into exile for the sake of Christ, and to preach His Gospel. To his disciples he said 'Let him be filled with God who wishes that his prayers may come true ... Blessed is the soul wounded by love, for in its wounding it is always healed'. He and his companions arrived first in Brittany. Such was the success of his mission to the pagans that King Sigebert of Austrasia gave him the use of a disused Roman fortress at Annegray, in the marshes and woods of the Vosges. Here he set up his first monastery. Thanks to the magnificent work of the French Association of the Friends of Saint Columban some thirty years

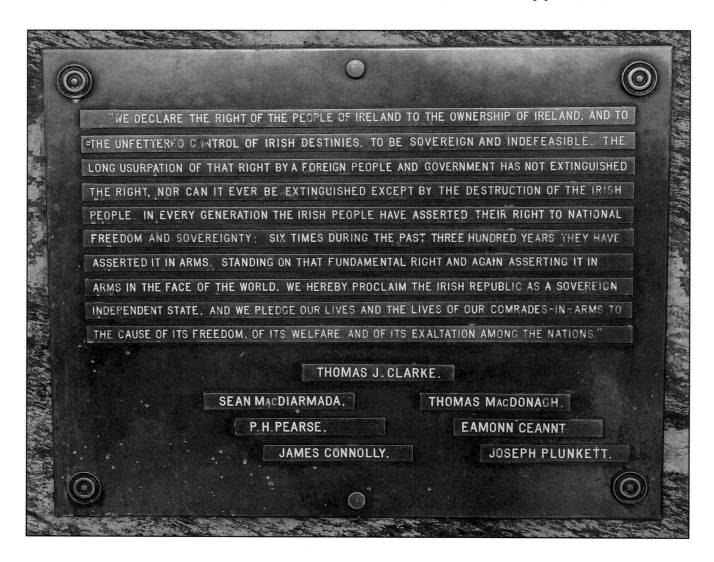

Above: a plaque bearing the declaration of the ring leaders of the 1916 Rising. All seven signatories of the Proclamation of the Irish Republic were executed by firing squad.

□
Prisons have played a large part in Irish history, and Kilmainham goal (left and below left), now open to the public as a museum, was the site of the execution of the leaders of the 1916 insurrection. Below: the Parnell Monument. Parnell was imprisoned in Kilmainham for his part in the Land League agitation of the nineteenth century.

□
Left: a simple monument commemorating the 1798 rising against the British near Collins Barracks. The year 1798 saw revolutions throughout Europe, and Ireland was no exception. The peasantry, goaded into revolution by the brutal excesses of the British military, were nevertheless no match for the troops.

The true flavour of the Dublin accent can be savoured in her fruit, flower and vegetable market stalls (these pages).

ago, excavations at Annegray have unearthed the actual foundations of the monastery and some seventh-century burial places, giving us a startling idea of the Spartan manner in which the monks of Columbanus lived.

The third foundation of the Saint, at Fontaines, is marked by his statue. From here he moved on to Luxeuil, and in a short time was reclaiming all Gaul for Christ. His territory had once been 'civilised' by the Romans, but had then fallen to the Vandals, the Goths and the Huns. While the Franks had embraced Christianity briefly, they had acquired only a veneer of religion over their barbarity. He then founded his monastery at Luxeuil, and then another at Fontaines. Luxeuil was a vast concern, and more than

☐ Patrick Kavannagh, the Monaghan poet, used to say that true Dubliners (this page) were those who did not have to go down to the country for their annual holidays.

However, most Dubliners come from any part of Ireland except Dublin – and Corkmen are said to predominate, particularly in top jobs.

just a religious way of life – it brought civilisation in its widest terms to Gaul, from literature to medicine. It was here that he wrote his marvellous prayer:

'Inspire us with Thy charity O Lord, that our loving quest for thee may occupy our every inmost thought: that Thy love may take complete possession of our being, and divine charity so fashion our senses that we may know not how to love anything else but thee.'

While at Luxeuil, Columbanus set out the rules of the monastic life as he saw it. First of all he laid down the general doctrines of the Church on which the monks were to base their lives, and the emphasis was on living out the life directed by the Gospels. Columban monks were to be marked by their obedience, silence, penance, poverty, prayer, prudence and

The women of Dublin are the dominant force in the market place (above), both as buyers and sellers, while their menfolk are liable to be pub philosophers over a 'pint of plain'.

Above: flower sellers in Dublin Market.

Above: the 'Long Room' of Trinity College. This first-floor room houses the library, where special displays are periodically arranged. Greene's Bookshop (left), between Trinity College and Merrion Square, is one of Dublin's most satisfactory for book browsers.

□ Below: Goldsmith's statue outside Trinity College. This eighteenth-century playwright spent four years at Trinity, running away at one point, but returning to graduate in 1749.

□ Top left, left and above: Greene's Bookshop. Dublin bookshops are some of the best in the world.

□
Right: crowds on Queen Maev Bridge and (remaining pictures) the Guinness Brewery, a castle of industry that looks almost romantic in the late afternoon light. Factory chimneys are an unusual sight in Dublin as the city lacks heavy industry.

chastity. Like Saint Francis of Assisi, Columbanus imparted to them a very great love of animals and birds. For him, squirrels came down from the trees and curled up in his cowl, and wolves accompanied him in the forests.

The sternness of his rule, exemplified by dawn-till-dusk prayer and work in the fields, offered the example of a cultivated manner of life to the Europeans. In his wisdom he created confessors – 'soul friends' for the faithful – and turned from public to private confession. Thus his main contribution was to the theology of penance. He was also ahead of his time in introducing frequent Communion. The rule of Saint Columbanus was basically the rule which prevailed in the Irish monastery of Bangor. It stood for prayer, physical labour and study, with fasting and asceticism as a background. Self-denial was the keynote and Irish monks did not take off on mystical 'highs'. They kept their bare feet firmly on the ground. The rule of Luxeuil, for example, lays down that food and drink should be frugal. A monk was advised to learn the virtues of humility, patience,

silence and gentleness from his brother monks. The weakness in this rule really lay in its penitentials. Practically every sin in the book had its corresponding years of penance, all set out in remarkable detail.

As Columbanus had no fear of dissolute kings and royalty, they experienced his wrath and he fell foul of them, ultimately being exiled from Luxeuil. He made for Bregenz on Lake Constance in Switzerland, but he was forced to move on again, crossing the Alps to Milan. In 614, at Bobbio, he founded his last and most famous monastery, and a year later, on 23rd November, he died there. This monastery, a great house of learning in Lombardy, was the centre of learning of Northern Italy, a furnace of prayer and an intellectual factory of science and teaching. Indeed, wherever Columbanus and his companions had wandered, monasteries had sprung up – for example, in the Brie County,

☐
The National Gallery of Ireland (above) was opened in 1864 and contains works from all major European schools, while the National Museum (right and facing page top left) houses one of the greatest gold collections in Europe and an impressive array of Irish antiquities.

□
The National Gallery (below) houses one of the best collections of old masters in the British Isles.

□
Above: Kilmainham Gaol, now a museum. At the entrance (left) to the National Gallery (below) stands a statue of Dargan, a railway pioneer.

This page: inhabitants of Dublin taking their ease.

Faremoutiers in the Seine and in Maine country at Rebais. Scores of Irish,
French and Italian followers came after him, living according to the
precepts of Columban rule.

After his death, his work was carried on by his disciples, among whom
were Saint Eustasius and Saint Walbert of Luxeuil, Saint Gall, who founded
the Abbey of Saint Gall in Switzerland, Saint Sisigbert who built Disentis;
Saint Valery, patron saint of gardeners, and Saint Faro of Sante-Croix.
There were numerous abbots who followed in his path, such as Ado of
Jouarre; Ouen of Rebais; Radon of Reuil; and dozens of bishops, among
them Amand of Maestricht, Arnould of Metz, Aubert of Cambrai, Chagnon
of Laon, Didier of Vienne, Donatus of Besançon, Eligius of Noyon,

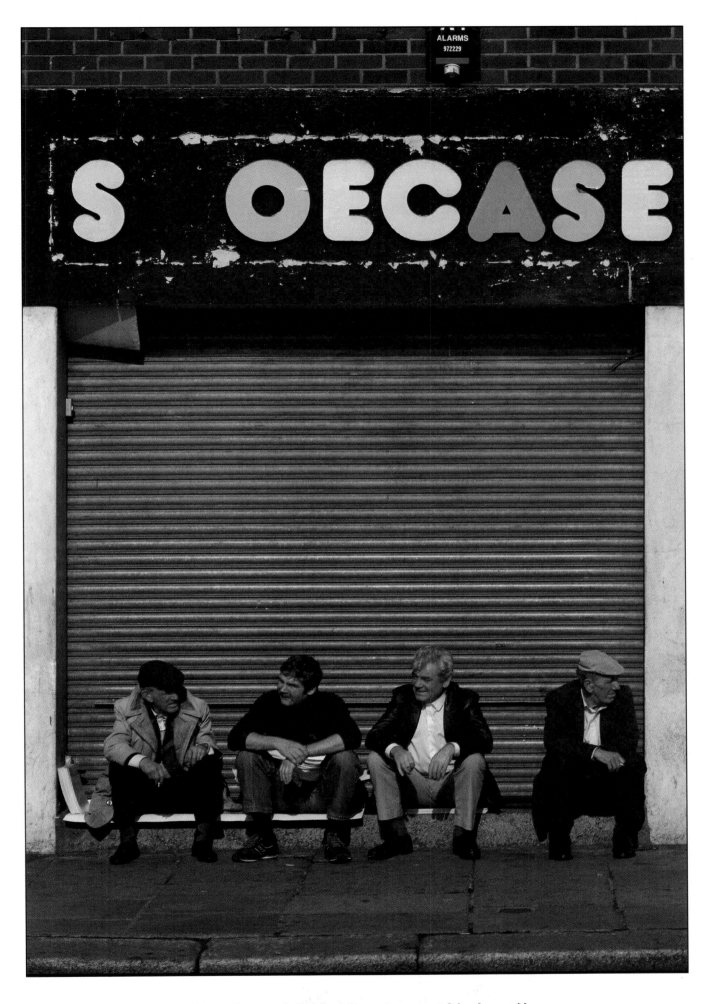

Above: the step of a Dublin shop serves as a seat. It has been said
that Ireland escapes an annual revolution – even though it has
high unemployment – because 30,000 people emigrate every year.

Above: the ornate ceiling
of the Royal Hospital's
chapel in Kilmainham
and (left) St Audoen's
Church, which dates from
the twelfth century and is
Dublin's oldest parish
church.

Left: St Michan's Church organ, played by Handel and (below) Christ Church Cathedral. Bottom: the sombre simplicity of the chapel at Kilmainham Gaol.

Ermenfroy of Verdun, and Léger of Autun – so many, in fact, that they read like a litany of the saints combined with a Michelin guide to France.

When you consider that Saint Columbanus was seventy years of age when he cleared a forest on the land given to him by Agilulph, King of the Lombards, to set up the monastery at Bobbio, you get some indication of the enormous physical strength as well as the great spiritual strength of this Irish saint. When the monastery was completed in 614 he was seventy three years of age.

The O'Connell Bridge (right) across the Liffey (below) is as broad as it is long, and is dominated by a statue of Daniel O'Connell.

His writings and admonitions are still applicable to the world of today. Many of them are profoundly moving – take, for example, this simple letter of admonition to his brother monks, written as he left the monastery at Luxeuil:

'I had at first meant to write a letter full of sorrows and fears, but knowing well that your heart is overwhelmed with cares and labours, I have changed my style, and sought to dry the tears rather than call them forth. I have permitted only gentleness to be seen outside, and chained down the grief in the depths of my soul. But my own tears begin to flow. I must drive them back, for it does not become a good soldier to weep in front of the battle. After all, this that has happened to us is nothing new. Is it not what we have preached everyday? Was there not of old a philosopher wiser than the others who was thrown into prison for holding against the opinion of all that there was only one God? The Gospels also are full of all that is necesssary to encourage us. They were written with that purpose,

☐
This page: Dublin street life. Buskers abound in Dublin, as in every European city, and do much to enhance the capital's charm.

☐
Above: Merchant's Alley. Dublin's alleyways are fast disappearing, though a few attractive ones still remain to house collections of tiny shops.

Marsh's Library (below) was founded in 1707 and is Ireland's oldest public library. Left: the National Gallery and (bottom) Trinity College.

to teach the true disciples of Christ crucified to follow Him wearing their cross. Our perils are many; the struggle that threatens us is severe, but the recompense is glorious, and the freedom of our choice is manifest. Without adversaries no conflict, and without conflict, no crown. Where the struggle is, there is courage, vigilance, patience, fidelity, wisdom, prudence, out of the fight there is misery and disaster. Thus then, without war no crown, and I add without freedom no honour.'

At the time of his death this indomitable Saint had every intention of embarking upon a mission to the Slavs. A French savant has summed up Saint Columbanus' life work thus:

☐
Right: the River Liffey, whose banks are graced by the eighteenth-century Four Courts (below). Designed by Thomas Cooley and built of granite and Portland stone, this beautiful building was begun in 1786.

☐
Above: the National Museum, where the surroundings are worthy of the exhibits. Right: Iveagh Market entrance.

'The light of Saint Columbanus, dissemminated by his knowledge and doctrine, wherever he presented himself, caused a writer of his time to compare him to the sun in his course from East to West: and he continued after his death to shine forth in numerous disciples whom he had trained in learning and sanctity.'

The work of Saint Columbanus in his life was sufficient to set Western Europe on fire with Christianity, but it was after his death that his influence was really felt. The men he trained as his disciples set up at least 105 monasteries, among which Bobbio, the Lombardy monastery, became a shining light in Europe for its learning. Much later, a French saint wrote:

'The apostolic zeal, which drove the monks of Ireland to the Continent, led Saint Columbanus to Bobbio, at the foot of the wild deserts of the Appenines. He bore to this place, along with the severe observances of the hermits of his country, their passion for letters, and the necessity

These pages: Iveagh Market. It is a sign of financially stressful times in Dublin that the Molly Malones and Biddy Mulligans are still obliged to search through such secondhand clothing markets for their apparel.

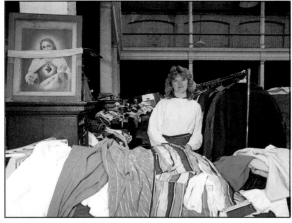

Either by night (this page) or by day (facing page top) Dublin is an attractive sight – a city of history cloaked in poetry.

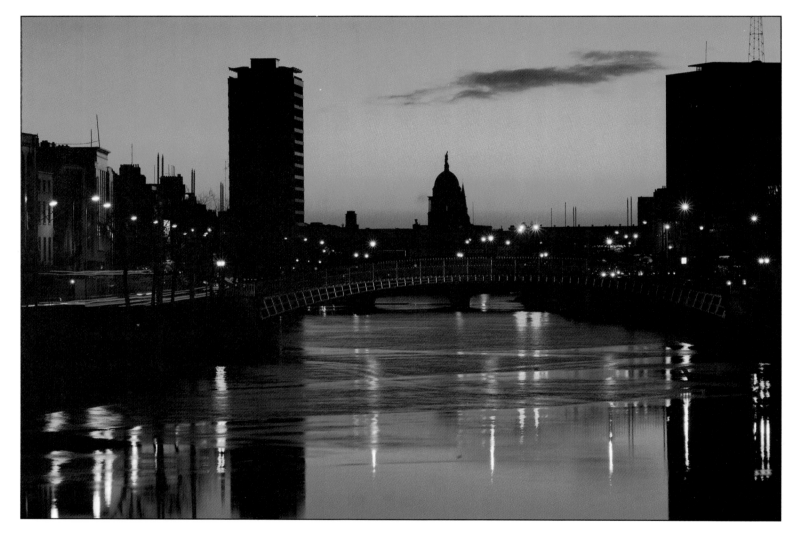

which possessed them for learning and teaching. The spirit of this great reformer lived after him and spread on from those Irishmen who were his companions to their Italian disciples and successors. He took on the profligate kings and princes of the decadent, post-barbaric period of European history and conquered them spiritually.'

Marguerite-Marie Dubois, one of the best-informed modern writers on Saint Columbanus, has this to say of the authenticity of the biography that the Piedmontese monk, Jonas, wrote of him:

'Jonas entered the monastery of Bobbio during the abbacy of Saint Attalen in 618, three years after the death of Saint Columbanus. He was the secretary and personal attendant of the Abbot, and collected memories of the founder's life from numerous witnesses, all of which are worthy of belief. He was also careful to cite his authorities and claimed his writings contained no fact for which he did not have reliable evidence.

After the death of Attalen, Jonas became the attendant of Saint Berthulf, whom he accompanied to Rome, in June 628, on a visit to Pope Honorius. It was on Saint Berthulf's suggestion that he wrote the *Life of Saint Columbanus*, in about the year 640. Jonas likewise wrote the biographies of Saint Eustatius, Saint Attalen, Saint Berthulf, Saint John of Récrué, Saint Farus and others as well. His desire to edify, his taste for the marvellous, a certain partiality for Irish monasticism – easy to understand – combined with a surprising ignorance of history and contemporary geography, prevents us from accepting all his assertions unreservedly. Nevertheless, it remains true that his work continues to be the best ground work for all the biographies of Saint Columbanus.'

We should not be too worried about Jonas' lack of geographical knowledge as we know, by way of contrast, that the Irish monk Saint

Above: (left) Queen Maev Bridge and (right) Heuston Bridge and station.

☐
The Dubliner (right) is as unique to his fair city as Cockneys are to London. Few of them are 'natives', though, the majority coming from the countryside, drawn to the big city by the hope of finding employment.

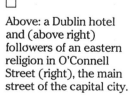

Above: a Dublin hotel and (above right) followers of an eastern religion in O'Connell Street (right), the main street of the capital city.

Below: a sleeping passenger on a Dublin bus. The national
transport company of Ireland is called C.I.E., *Corus Lanpuir
Eirean*, which Dubliners freely translate as 'Chassis In Excelsis'.

Fearghal was teaching that the earth was round, and that it had north and
south poles, when no one – not even the great Saint Boniface, the Apostle
of Germany – believed him.

We can, of course, add to knowledge of the Saint gleaned from Jonas' *Life
of Saint Columbanus* by reading what he actually wrote himself – his
Regula Monachorum, his *Regula Coenobialis*, his sermons, his letters, and
his poetry. In this way we know almost as much about him as we do, say,
about Winston Churchill in our time.

Followers of Saint Columbanus who continued the spread of learning and
the gospels included Saint Ursan, who made his way to the Bernese Jura
and built there the Abbey of Saint Ursan in the lowlands below Mont
Terrible. Saint Gall, companion of Saint Columbanus and, like him, a
Leinster man, became the patron Saint of Switzerland. The town of Saint
Gallis is in the middle of the Swiss canton of that name, and is also the
name of the diocese. His influence radiated from here to
Germany and Austria.

Today, one can find dozens of parish churches dedicated to Saint Gall, the
saint from Leinster. He was a strongly documented historical character –
our friend Walafrido Strabo wrote about him, as did Jonas. Saint Gall had a
rough time among the pagan Germanic tribes, in particular the Alemans.
One of the many stories told about him is that he miraculously blew up an
enormous barrel of beer which the Germans were about to offer as a
sacrifice to their god Wodan. Saint Gall operated around Brigantua, at

Trinity College (below and bottom) – to give it its full title, 'the College of the Holy and Undivided Trinity' – was founded in 1591 by Queen Elizabeth I.

Above: Marsh Library, which remains much as it was when it was first built. Its darkened oak shelves contain some 25,000 beautifully bound volumes, including Dean Swift's copy of Clarendon's *History of the Great Rebellion*. Facing page: the marble interior of Dublin's City Hall, on Dame Street.

Gaelic football (below), the national game of Ireland, holds its final before vast crowds in Croke Park, Dublin. Finalists stand a good chance of meeting again in local or national politics and are certain of everlasting national glory.

Lake Constance, where he was, for a considerable time, a very sick man. By the sheer holiness of his monastic life in his cell, he radiated Christianity. When they wanted to make him a bishop, he declined, allowing one of his monks the honour of being made Bishop of Constance. He was offered the abbacy of Luxeil, but refused this too as he foresaw his approaching death.

He died while visiting his priest friend, Willimar, at Arbon on the south shore of Lake Constance, and his body was brought back to the monastery which now bears his name. Ironically, the monastery of Saint Gall, a follower of the rule of Saint Columbanus, became a Benedictine monastery in 720. His remains now lie in state in the monastic church, today the cathedral of the diocese of Saint Gall. The building standing today was rebuilt in the late 1700s and its chapel devoted to the Irish Saint.

Saint Sigisbert, disciple of Saint Columbanus, founded the monastery of Disentis in the Chur district of Rhaectia, near the source of the Rhine. When Saint Columbanus died, Saint Attala, a nobleman and a Burgundian, took over the monastery at Bobbio. After his death, his place was taken by a young Frankish monk, Bertulf, who had Bobbio placed under the personal guidance of Pope Honorius. The Pope was so struck by the rule of Saint Columbanus at Bobbio that he exempted it from the authority of any bishop.

Ireland, despite its small population, turns out a fair quota of athletes (below left), including Olympic gold medalists. Events such as the Dublin Marathon (left) attract thousands of runners.

Above: an Irish piper. Left: the Nissan Bicycling Race. Cycling is a national pastime in Ireland, and in recent years some champion Irish cyclists have won the prestigious French cycling championships.

Right: a lock on the
Grand Canal (bottom),
which describes a huge
arc from the west of the
city to Grand Canal
Docks in the east. Below:
a summer's afternoon in
Phoenix Park.

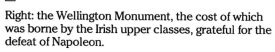

Right: the Wellington Monument, the cost of which
was borne by the Irish upper classes, grateful for the
defeat of Napoleon.

Below: fallow deer in
Phoenix Park (right),
which lies at the western
entrance to the city and
is one of the largest
public parks in the world,
covering 1,760 acres.

In general the saints and scholars of Ireland's Golden Age lacked spiritual
arrogance. Each one knew in his heart of hearts the saying of the national
apostle of Ireland, Saint Patrick. He had said:

'I was like a stone lying deep in the mud until He who is mighty came and
in all His mercy lifted me up and placed me on top of the wall. May it
never befall me from my God that I should lose his people whom he has
purchased at the ends of the earth. A hundred times in the day I prayed
and a hundred times in the night I rose to pray.'

Of all the famous scholars in this Island of Saints and Scholars, after the
great Saint Colmcille, and that colossus of monastic life, Saint
Columbanus, the 'supremo' was surely Saint Fearghal, who became more
commonly known as 'Virgil', Bishop of Salzburg. Scholar, reformer,
preacher, administrator and bishop, he was one of the very few Irish saints
who was not declared such by public demand, but was formally

canonised in Rome by a Pope, Gregory IX, with all its attendant pomp and circumstance. It took five hundred years for this due process to come about, presumably because after all was said and done, he was only an Irish monk. He died in 784. When Rome declared him Saint 'Virgil', or 'Virgilius', most people had forgotten that he was originally Fearghal, Irish Abbot of Aghaboe – 'Achadh Bo' – the Irish for 'The Field of the Cow', in County Laois in the province of Leinster. A Church of Ireland parish church now stands on the site of the original monastery.

Fearghal was primarily a mathematician, far in advance of his time. He headed for the Continent as an exile for Christ, meeting with King Pippin the Short at his court in Quierzy on the River Oise in 741. The then baby son of Pippin was destined to become the famous Charlemagne. The French king cultivated the friendship of Fearghal and after a year or two persuaded him to go to Bavaria where a revolt by the Duke of Bavaria had been put down. This was a classic example of the 'neutral' Irishman being used as a Christian emissary when a Frank or an Anglo-Saxon would have been suspected of personal bias.

Fearghal, abbot of the monastery of Saint Peter, was now made Bishop of Salzburg. Unfortunately for Anglo-Irish relations, Saint Boniface, an English saint from Devon, did not much care for this development. Fearghal was a monk-priest-abbot made bishop by a neighbouring Irish bishop, Dub Dá Crích. This appointment was an old Irish custom of which Saint Boniface did not approve and he had the full backing of Pope Zacharias in Rome. After all, horror of horrors, the mathematical Fearghal

The Hill of Howth, 560 feet high, forms the northern arm of Dublin Bay, nine miles from the centre of Dublin city. Its summit, overlooking the little fishing harbour (above), offers magnificent panoramic views.

Baltriggan (above), twenty miles west of Dublin, is a quiet seaside
resort with sheltered, sandy beaches. The town was famed for its
hosiery, and for its 'Balbriggans', the Victorian 'Long Johns'.

☐
Right: North Bull Island, a
three-mile-long sandbank
that runs parallel to the
northern shores of Dublin
Bay. Seafood restaurants
are good and plentiful on
these shores, particularly
in Howth (remaining
pictures).

believed and taught that the earth was round, and not only round, but that it had north and south poles! Such scholarship in the eighth century sent the 'flat-earther' Pope Zacharias into a spin, and he wrote to his fellow flat-earther, Saint Boniface, suggesting that this monk, if indeed he was a priest at all, was 'straying away from Catholic doctrine' and that 'his perverse and wicked doctrine' was in 'opposition to God'. Fearghal had far too brilliant a mind to be trapped into excommunication, and instead derived a certain amount of amusement by taking on Saint Boniface and the Pope in scientific disputations. After all, Fearghal came from a land where the pagan Celts in passage-graves, such as that at Newgrange in County Meath, had been plotting the path of the sun, moon and stars, albeit primitively, since 2,500 B.C. These very early astronomers had used their knowledge to set the pattern of dates for sowing crops and marking of the seasons of the year.

Such was Fearghal's sense of fun that he wrote, under a *nom de plume*, a treatise on cosmography, which he attributed to Saint Jerome, and which was taken seriously. His monks founded other monasteries, including those at Innichen and Kremsmünster. Fearghal died on 27th November, 784, and was buried in his cathedral at Salzburg. He had been the first Irish mathematician of European stature. Incidentally, the most notable Irish mathematician in the nineteenth century was Sir William Rowan Hamilton who subscribed to the quantum theory and the concept of the quaternian. He is said to have scratched the basic formula of quaternious on the stone of a canal bridge as he strolled through Dublin, deep in thought. In the twentith century, President Eamon De Valera, a former professor of

Howth (above) was a favourite haunt of James Joyce, as well as other Irish writers, poets and painters. On the Hill of Howth stands the home of Ireland's outstanding political thinker and writer, Dr Connor Cruise O'Brien.

Facing page: Trim Castle, Trim and (below) Headfort mansion at Ceanannus Mor. Right and bottom: a race meeting on the strand at Laytown.

mathematics, was said to be the only academic in Dublin's Institute of Advanced Studies who understood Einstein's Theory of Relativity. As Irish scholars, Sir William Rowan Hamilton and Eamon De Valera were worthy successors to Fearghal.

In the field of geography the most eminent Irish monk scholar of the time was the seventh-century saint, Dicuil (or Deicola), Abbot of Bosham. He received his initial training at the monastic university of Clonmacnoise on the banks of the River Shannon. His *De Mensuria Orbis Terrarum* was the first book in the world to mention the existence of Iceland. He collected all the geographical works existing in Greek and Latin and checked them against the reports of experienced Irish traveller-monks, eventually

*'A terrible and splendid trust
Heartens the host of Innisfail:
Their dream is of the swift sword-thrust,
A lightning glory of the Gael.*

*Croagh Patrick is the place of prayers,
And Tara the assembly place:
But each sweet wind of Ireland bears
The trump of battle on its race.'*

(Lionel Johnson 1867-1902)

compiling a fairly accurate account of lands from the Faroe Islands to the banks of the Nile.

Dungal, an Irish monk from the monastic university at Bangor, was the most distinguished astronomer in Europe in the ninth century. He was head of the great school of Pavia, later to become one of the best known universities in northern Italy. In 810 he wrote a detailed explanation of a double eclipse of the sun for Charlemagne, while in 855, Sedulius the Younger, an Irish monk of Liège, wrote his *De Rectoribus Christianis* – the first attempt to set out the duties of a Christian king. It was a treatise on the theory of political government, far in advance of its time, directed at the sovereign Lothair the Second, and it pointed the way for treatises by Saint Thomas of Colona and Dante on the same subject.

The learning of these monk-pilgrims culminates in the greatest of Irish thinkers, John Scotus Eriugena, who was born in Ireland in 807. John

Facing page: (top) the ruins of the Abbey Church on the Hill of
Slane, and (bottom) Newgrange, the burial place of the Kings of
Tara. Below: the Hill of Tara, where Saint Patrick lit the first
Paschal Fire.

'In a quiet water'd land, a land of roses,
Stands Saint Kieran's city fair;
And the warriors of Erin in their famous generations
Slumber there.
There beneath the dewy hillside sleep the noblest
Of the clan of Conn,
Each below his stone with name in branching Ogham
And the sacred knot thereon.

There they laid to rest the seven Kings of Tara,
There the sons of Cairbré sleep –
Battle-banners of the Gael that in Kieran's plain
Of crosses
Now their final hosting keep.'

(T.W. Rolleston 1857-1920
– from the Irish of Angus O Gillan)

☐
Below: bales of straw await collection in a field below Slievenaglogh, and (right) a wrecked ship, deserted by the tide, lies on a beach near Baltray.

☐
Above: the magnificent interior of Westport House, which belongs to the Marquis of Sligo, and (right) the Round Tower at Monasterboice, part of the ruins of the fifth-century monastery founded by St Buithe.

Scotus was at the court of Charles the Bald in Laon in northern France from 845, and Charles wisely put him in charge of the palace school. Here again was an example of an Irish monk who had a mastery of Greek and Latin. He translated the works of Dionysius the Areopagite, who was converted by Saint Paul in Athens, of Maximus Confessor and of Gregory of Nysssa, opening a new window on European thought with a blast of Eastern theology. He is best remembered for the five volumes of his *De Divisione Natural*, published in 867. A controversial thinker, way ahead of his time, he was accused of being a Neo-Platonist. His influence was so great that it became fashionable for discussions in Laon to take place in Greek. In fact, a knowledge of Greek was the hallmark of an Irish monk-scholar. John Scotus' encyclopaedic knowledge of the classics was passed on to his fellow Irish monks and companions.

However novel the Pope might think these Greek-speaking Irish monk scholars, his Holiness could never fault them as heretics, as they always

☐
Above: Proleek Dolman at Ballymascanlan. It is said to be lucky to throw a stone that remains on the capstone. Left: Dundalk Bay as seen from Shelling Hill Beach.

Below: Slieve Gullion Forest Park. Slieve Gullion is Armagh's
highest mountain, attaining nearly 2,000 feet. On its southern peak
stands a prehistoric passage grave.

stayed close to the Scriptures – which came to them in the purer form of
Greek rather than Latin – and they remained loyal to the teachings of the
Fathers of the Church, in particular to the great Saint Augustine. The Irish
scholar-monks were thus in the mainstream of orthodox Catholic
teachers, thinkers and writers.

The primacy of Peter was an integral part of the Christian faith which the
Irish monks brought with them to Europe. It was a faith which was
characterised by a devotion to Saint Peter and the popes, his successors
in Rome. Nevertheless, Irish monastic discipline concentrated on the
pastoral care of the people they converted. Cut off from the European
mainstream, they were not concerned with diocesan bishoprics and the
details of ecclesiastical provinces. Their spiritual world was based on their
monastery – the hierarchical system belonged to the Continentals.
Eventually, new religious orders and a system of regular dioceses took
over where the Irish monks left off, but it was not until Norman times that
Ireland divided itself up into four archbishoprics and their suffragan sees
under a cardinal papal legate from Rome. The early Irish monk-
missionaries sought spiritual power only, avoiding temporal power
whenever possible.

□

Above: Gosford Castle in autumn, an apparently Norman castle which was built in the nineteenth century and stands near Markethill. Left: a view of a slate grey Lough Neagh from Oxford Island, near the lough's south shore.

Arguably the most splendid relic of Irish monastic life is the monastery of bee-hive cells still standing on the most isolated rock in Europe, Skellig Michael. This island is one of three little pinnacles known as the Skelligs that lie off the coast of County Kerry. Skellig Michael is difficult to approach in heavy seas – the huge mass of steep, slate rock, less than a half-mile long and a quarter-of-a-mile wide, rises sheer out of the water to over 700 feet in height. The ruins of the Abbey stand over 500 feet up from the crude landing stage.

There is one small, green patch around the stark, grey rocks called 'Christ's Saddle'. On a second plateau above are five bee-hive-shaped stone cells and a tiny oratory perched on top of the precipitous cliff. At a lower level stands a sixth bee-hive cell, a second little chapel, stone crosses, some burial places of the monks and a holy well. In the end, the

Vikings in their long boats came and murdered the monks and pillaged their chapels – and yet, ironically, it is said that the Norse king, Olaf, was baptised by a monk on Skellig Michael. Today the island is uninhabited by human souls, a haunt of myriad rare seabirds, including fulmar petrels, kittiwake gulls, puffins, choughs, guillemots, peregrine falcons and even stormy petrels. Surveying the scene now, it is easy to agree with the remark made by Sir Kenneth Clark at the beginning of his television series *Civilisation:*

'Looking back from the giant civilisations of twelth-century France or seventeenth-century Rome, it is hard to believe that for quite a long time Western Christianity survived by clinging on to places like Skellig Michael.'

A sharp contrast to life on the Skelligs in the turbulent waters of the Atlantic Ocean was to be found in the vast monastic universities on the mainland, such as those at Kells, Bangor and Clonmacnoise. Here hundreds of bee-hive cells housed the monk-students and teachers.

□

Probably one of the best known Irish ballads is 'The Mountains of Mourne', and these mountains (facing page) are worthy of the honour. The range sweeps down to the sea in County Down, extending for almost fifteen miles between Dundrum Bay and Carlingford Lough. Above: the view looking east from Crocknafeola Wood at the foot of the Mourne Mountains (above right and right).

'I follow the silver spears flung from the hands of dawn,
Through silence, through singing stars, I journey on and on:
The scattered fires of the sun, blown wide ere the day be done,
Scorch me hurrying after the swift white feet of my fawn.'

(Ethua Carberry 1866-1902)

□
On Scrabo Hill, near the Georgian town
of Newtownards, stands a tower (left)
erected in memory of a Marquis of
Londonderry. As the surrounding
countryside (top and above) is
comparatively flat, this landmark can be
seen for miles.

Equipped with simple stone chapels and kitchens, these monasteries also had an unique Celtic architectural defence against the raiding Vikings, the hundred-foot-high round tower. With its entrance many feet above the ground, this served as both a watch tower and an alarm tower when the dreaded longboats of the Vikings were seen coming up the estuaries on hit-and-run plundering raids. On these occasions, the monks would scatter, and their precious altar pieces and illuminated manuscripts would be stored in the tower, the entrance ladder being pulled in to await the departure of the raiders. As it had no corners it was impossible for the raiders to breach the tower.

The monks of Skellig Michael and of the mainland monastic universities had a deep love of nature. Like the hero Finn of the ancient Irish saga, the *Fianna*, they loved music, which, to him and to them, was the song of the blackbird, the scream of an eagle, the roar of a waterfall and the baying of hounds. Unlike many lovers of sagas, the Irish monks did not merely remain content with ephemeral music. They believed, as did the poet and dreamer of dreams, Oisin, that the music which delighted them best was 'the music of the thing that happens', for they were men of action as well as dreamers.

Lest we think that Irish monasticism lived only in heady ethereal dreams, we are reminded of their great artistry in a wealth of Irish manuscripts, such as those within the Book of Kells and the Book of Durrow, two of the most valuable books in the world. These are Byzantine in character, their iconography shot through with Eastern associations, reflecting the influence of Syria and the Coptic lands, but the unique Irish script was a cultural phenomenon.

□
Cushendun (facing page), near the mouth of the Glendun River, is a famous Antrim beauty spot. Above: Glenriff Forest Park Nature Reserve and (above right) the view looking north from Ballygalley. County Antrim, in the northeast corner of Ireland, is only thirteen miles from the Scottish coast. The county can boast, arguably, the most beautiful coastal road (right) in the whole of Ireland.

Below: mist and sea pinks cloak the cliffs at White Rocks.

□
Left: Carrickfergus Castle, where even the portcullis remains intact. Below: Dunluce Castle and (bottom) Carnlough Bay.

In the history of illuminated manuscripts there has been nothing to equal this script. There is nothing 'Celtic Twilighty' or twee about the bold calligraphy and illumination of books such as the Stowe Missal, the Book of the Dun Cow, or the Book of Armagh. Like the Celtic Christianity they portrayed, the manuscripts are clear, intense and definitive. Their sole purpose was to show the reader the Word of God, the Gospels, and the scribes had a lot of fun in so doing. Spirals, trumpets, La Téne curvilinear motifs and patterns, and fantastic and exotic animals abounded in their texts of the Gospels. Snakes, eagles, calves, and lions are there, all depicted by the monks in the most beautiful colour combinations – those of the real world around them – vermilion red, green, yellow, brown and black. As a consequence, these Irish manuscripts are among the most original and animated in the history of calligraphy.

□
Cushendall (right), situated at the northern
end of Red Bay, is an ideal spot from which
to explore the Glens of Antrim. Below:
Larne, whose proximity to Scotland means
that the route from here is the shortest sea
passage across the Irish Sea.

The Giant's Causeway (above) is one of the most
fascinating ancient rock formations in the world. It was
formed when molten larva burst through the earth's
crust and cooled over a large area. The resulting basalt
rocks rise in hexagonal columns.

☐
Right: Glendun, 'the glen of the fort', one of the picturesque Nine Glens of Antrim. This is the country of Shane O'Neill, Sir Roger Casement and the clan MacDonnell.

☐
Above: landscape near Aldergrove Airport. Slemish Mountain (right), 1,437 feet high, is traditionally associated with St Patrick's youth as a slave.

Below: Wishing Arch, near Portrush, which is one of the most
favoured holiday resorts in the country. The Antrim coast, from
Belfast to Portrush, is renowned throughout Ireland for its beauty.

The humanity of the illuminators and scribes is often evident in their
work. One can see, for example, among the words on a line in the Book of
Kells a 'doodle' of a bumble bee. Here, within these pages of sacred texts,
a monastic cat watches a monastic mouse, a dog stretches, a cock struts.
Sometimes a little margin entry illuminates the history of the time like a
lightning flash. Here is a note written during the days of the plundering of
Irish monasteries by the Norse raiders:

'Fierce and wild is the wind tonight,
It tosses the tresses of the sea to white;
On such a night as this I take my ease;
Fierce Norsemen only course the quiet seas.'

In the margins of some of the most beautiful Celtic manuscripts in the
world are the musings of some of the Celtic scribes. Two rare examples
are as follows:

'A dinnerless Tuesday is a cold thing, Donall, and immediately before
Christmas too.'

And another,

'My hand is weary with writing, my sharp quill is not steady, my slender,
beaked pen juts forth a black draught of shining, dark blue ink, a stream of
the wisdom of Blessed God'

☐
Right: the seemingly
fragile rope bridge at
Carrick-a-Rede. This is
taken down in winter –
even the locals will not
cross then! Below: a
waterfall in Glenariff, one
of the more famous of
the Glens of Antrim.

☐
Above: north Antrim coast, and (right) a lane snakes
down to the sea north of Ballintoy.

The Giant's Causeway
(this page), geologically
one of the wonders of the
world, is, at first sight, a
little disappointing as it is
not 'gigantic' in scale, but
rather small. Its three
main outcrops of lava
rocks are called the Little
Causeway, the Middle
Causeway and the Grand
Causeway.

Besotted by the natural world all around them, the Irish monk-scribes
recorded it in depictions of leaping salmon, an otter making off with a fish
in its mouth, or the play of light and shadow. Says one margin doodle,
'Pleasant is the glint of the sun today upon these margins, because
it flickers so.'

A glimpse of a monk in his cell working on an illuminated manuscript can
be seen in a poem by an anonymous Irish monk which, in English
translation, says:

'I and Pangur Bán, my cat,
'Tis a like task we are at;
Hunting mice is his delight,
Hunting words I sit all night.

'The great Gaels of Ireland
Are the men that God made mad,
For all their wars are merry
And all their songs are sad.'

(G.K. Chesterton 1874-1936)

Facing page: the ruin of Kenbane Castle overlooks the North
Channel. Below: the north coast road near the Giant's Causeway.

Better far than praise of men
'Tis to sit with book and pen;
Pangur bears me no ill-will,
He, too plies his simple skill ...'

Time and time again oval-eyed saints gaze out at you from the pages of
the Book of Kells. Christ and His mother are depicted in styles from the
Byzantine Empire, from Coptic Egypt or from Ethiopia – Celtic icons
touching hands with the East. The illustrations and calligraphy reflect the
sparkling waters of the Aegean Sea and the dazzling sunlight of the Greek
Islands. Of this great book it could be said that a 'terrible beauty' was
born; and that that beauty shone with the elemental message of Saint
Paul, 'I live now, not I, but Christ livest in me.'

The Book of Kells, written in Latin, contains the four Gospels, plus
prefaces to some of them, a few little summaries, and some explanations
of Hebraic names. The pages are either of parchment or vellum, and
originally were gloriously ragged and uneven until some fool, God knows

who, cut the pages straight. Experts consider it unlikely that the whole book was the work of one single monk – it is more probable that four monks had a hand in its production.

The most famous page of all three hundred and forty – there are some pages missing, at the beginning and at the end – is the *Chi Rho* page, the Greek letters for the abbreviated form of the word Christ. On this page the 'doodle' is a portrayal of cats and mice, the cats watching two mice nibbling crumbs of bread. The often-reproduced portrait of the barefoot Christ has purple and royal peacocks to the left and right of his shoulders, alongside chalices and vines. One page has the traditional angel of Saint Matthew, the lion of Saint Mark, the ox of Saint Luke and the eagle of Saint John.

□
Top: wet sand seems as smooth as satin at Castlerock, while nearby Downhill Strand (left) is almost as white as the surf. Above: Binevenagh.

☐
Below: a rock pool on Castlerock Beach and (right) Mussenden Temple, near Downhill, built by an eccentric bishop in 1783.

☐
Above: Portstewart basks in sunshine and (right) sheep graze at the eastern end of Glenelly Valley.

The portrait of the arrest of Christ shows two oval-eyed, red-headed men
with black beards seizing Him by the arms while, in an extraordinarily
grotesque arch overhead, two terrifying, snarling dogs confront each
other, while the face of the bearded Christ stares at you with a simple and
penetrating gaze from a powerful and, at the same time, humble face. The
blue eyes of the red-bearded, bare-foot Christ also look straight at you
from the page of the Apprehension. Here, his red robe over a blue
garment with Celtic 'trews', is like the chasuble of the priest celebrating
Mass. Up-raised arms are the classic pose of the priest – the *altar Christus*
– who traditionally maintains this position during the prayers of the most
sacred portion of the celebration of the Eucharist. The figure to the left
holds His right arm lightly with two hands, the figure to the right holds His
left arm almost symbolically. Both apprehending figures appear to be as
light and as in effectual in their efforts as ballet dancers.

The massive figure of Christ is cosmic, dominating the expanding universe. His raised arms remind a finite world that the crucifixion is to come, and that those same raised arms will also be those of the risen Christ of the Nicene Creed –

'On the third day He rose again
in accordance with the Scriptures,
He ascended into Heaven
and is seated at the right hand of the Father.
He will come again in glory to judge the living and the dead,
and His Kingdom will have no end.'

The whole page proclaims that Christ is an innocent victim offering himself voluntarily for the salvation of the world.

While the Book of Kells is generally thought to be of the eighth or ninth centuries, it is just possible that it is of an earlier century. The main clue,

□
Facing page: an aerial view of Drum Major Forest Park in autumn. Right: a summer's afternoon, and (above) evening, in Glenelly Valley. Above right: one of many rushing woodland streams to be found in Gortin Glen Forest Park, north of the town of Omagh.

Below right and below left: fishing boat repair in the little town of
Killybegs on Donegal Bay (bottom). The town has a fine natural
harbour and hospitable Gaelic people.

say the experts, is in the detail of an Irish warrior in the genealogy of Saint
Luke, who is depicted with a short, stabbing spear and a small, round
shield, which would suggest that he was an Irish warrior
of pre-Viking times.

It is called the Book of Kells because it was found in Kells in County
Meath, where there was once a famous abbey. It is possible that the work
was started by Irish monks in the monastery of Iona, and then brought to
Kells from there by the followers of Saint Colmcille when the Vikings
forced them to flee. Held in the safety of the parish church of Kells, the
book was removed to the Library of the College of the Holy and Undivided
Trinity in Dublin for safe-keeping during the destructive rule of Cromwell.
It can still be found there today.

Left: sorting out the nets in a Donegal village. Donegal, the most northeastern county in Ireland, is famous for its magnificent Atlantic coast, breathtaking mountain scenery and beautiful women.

While Killybegs (above right and right) is famous for its deep-sea fishing, Kilcar, just eight miles to the west, is famous for its handwoven tweed, embroidery and knitwear. The drive from Killybegs through Ardara, Dungloe and Gweedore to Portnablagh is incredibly beautiful, but, as yet, little known.

But to return to our Irish monk-missionaries in exile for Christ. While the spiritual conquest of Scotland is to the credit of the Irish monk Saint Colmcille, the major portion of the spiritual conquest of England has to be attributed to one of the most humble of Irish monks, Saint Aidan of Iona.

King Oswald, who had been baptized by the monks of Iona and wished to see Christianity restored to England, asked the Abbot of Iona to recommend a likely choice to lead this conversion. The Abbot had no hesitation in appointing Aidan, who was then made a bishop. Aidan chose as the 'launching pad' for his spiritual conquest of England the tiny island of Lindisfarne, just off the coast of Northumberland, and across from the King's royal residence of Bamburgh. The monastery which grew up at Lindisfarne became a major powerhouse of spiritual renewal and from it stemmed many other successful monastic foundations. Though we know nothing about his Irish roots, Saint Aidan had the good fortune to have that extraordinary English historian, the Venerable Bede, include him in the third volume of his five volumes of *Historia Ecclesiastica*. Possibly the English Saint Bede was more concerned with the history of King Oswald, but the lives of both were so intertwined that to relate one was to document the other.

The Venerable Bede was born in 670, within nineteen years of the death of Aidan, and his history of Aidan came from the men who had served the Bishop. When Bede wrote, the work of the Irish missionaries was more or less over, and on its very strong Celtic foundations had arisen a Roman church. In Bede's time, the Roman church in Anglo-Saxon Northumbria

Old farming ways (above) die hard, particularly in Donegal, where land holdings are extremely small, and people take a pride in keeping their farms neat and tidy.

□

Below: milking in the field and (right) rounding up a stray calf on the beach at Rossnowlagh.

□

Above: sheep are few and far between around the Gap of Mamore. Left: haymaking as the rain holds off. Donegal is predominantly the county of the clan O'Donnell, their greatest hero being Red Hugh, who repeatedly defeated the English armies in the sixteenth century.

☐
Lough Swilly (left and below), a fjord which sweeps inland for twenty-five miles, is famous as the landing place of the French battleships in 1798. Bottom: farming in the Gap of Mamore.

blossomed into a great and permanent establishment. The Venerable Bede describes in his *Historia Ecclesiastica* the founding of Lindisfarne thus:

'On the arrival of the bishop, the King granted him the land for which he was asking, on the island of Lindisfarne, where he could establish his episcopal see. The place in question, moreover, is an island twice a day, according to the tides, and is twice a day connected directly with the mainland. Then the King, accepting humbly and with a good will the orders given by Saint Aidan, showed great zeal in helping to build up the Church of Christ in his kingdom and in caring for it thereafter …'

The 'build up' of this Christian kingdom was to spread from the monastery of Lindisfarne to monasteries at Ripon, Whitby, Lastingham, Mailros, Saint-Bees and as far afield as Burgh Castle in East Anglia, Bosham in Sussex and Malmesbury.

The famous Book of Durrow was probably written on Lindisfarne. Lindisfarne writings developed a specific style, a zoomorphic pattern, brilliant in colours, akin to very early stained-glass work. The Lindisfarne Gospels – another superb collection of illuminated manuscripts – originated here and were for practical use in the church. They can be seen in the British Museum in London today.

The conversion of the pagan peoples of England was carried out in turbulent and warlike times, in a country under the constant threat of incursions and invasions and suffering frequent local battles and killings. Saint Aidan was basically a recluse, a hermit, a solitary mystic at prayer, during all this. Unlike many who were to come after him, the saint's main

Top left and top right: serious faces at a cattle auction, and (above) turf cutters digging fuel for the winter. Right: snug in the heather, sheep chew the cud on the Gap of Mamore.

virtue was total humility. He refused to ride a horse – that was for the Establishment – and the regime in his monastery was frugal. Kings, commoners and slaves were all equal in his eyes and treated as such. Royal patronage he avoided, except for the original grant of land, and the occasional use of King Oswald as an interpreter. He himself lived in abject poverty, detaching himself from possessions and worldly impedimenta. When King Oswald died, Aidan had the equal support of his successor, King Oiswin. There is a story that King Oiswin of Deira gave Saint Aidan a costly horse to help him in crossing rivers. Aidan promptly gave the animal to a poor beggar seeking aid. The King was, reasonably enough, annoyed, and when he raised the matter, Aidan asked him if he held the son of a mare dearer than the Son of God! Not long after this incident

☐ Facing page: set amid a patchwork of straight-sided fields, the Beltany Stone Circle forms a perfect ring. Lough Derg is famous for St Patrick's Purgatory (below). Here pilgrims fast for three days and two nights, go bare foot over the stones and repent of their sins – a tough, rough, mediaeval-style pilgrimage. Right: a view of Trawbreaga Bay from Drumaville and (below right) drystone walls dissect pasture at Maghery, near Dungloe.

Aidan died at Bamburgh. He died standing up, leaning against a wooden post in a make-shift shelter which had been erected against the wall of his church. He was buried in Lindisfarne.

The Venerable Bede portrayed Aidan's prayerful life, his humility and his devotion to the poor as a model for English bishops who were, at this time, beginning to get exaggerated ideas of their importance. He said of the saint:

'He neither sought after nor cared for worldly possessions but he rejoiced to hand over at once, to any poor man he met, the gifts which he had received from kings or rich men of the world. He used to travel everywhere, in town and country, not on horseback but on foot, unless compelled by urgent necessity to do otherwise, in order that, as he walked along, whenever he saw people whether rich or poor, he might at once approach them and, if they were unbelievers, invite them to accept

□ Top: ploughed fields draw the eye west over the view from the Grianan of Aileach. Above: a ruined farmhouse in the Urnis Hills and (right) scything by hand on a Donegal smallholding (facing page).

the mystery of faith or if they were believers, that he might strengthen them in the faith, urging them by word and deed to practise almsgiving and good works.'

In his works Bede frequently associated Aidan with events at the court of the kings. In fact Aidan was far from being a courtier, he was the very opposite and loathed the wine-swilling of the Anglo-Saxon soldiery and their gluttonous royal banquets, where the tables always groaned with food and drink. Similarly, Irish monk-missionaries of the present day are apt to share the poverty of the Third World, thus carrying on the Saint's tradition.

By comparison with the Roman Church, whose missions concentrated on city-dwellers, Aidan was typical, as a member of the Celtic Church, in

taking the Christian message to rural populations. After his death, the Irish and Roman churches came together and bishops were given permanent dioceses with limited borders. Consequently, wandering bishops became less frequent sights.

John Henry Newman, the saintly English cardinal who established the Catholic University of Dublin, regarded this 'Island of Saints and Scholars' during the Dark Ages as Christianity's 'storehouse of knowledge'. He had this to say of the influence of the Irish saints and scholars in his native land:

'O memorable time, when Saint Aidan and the Irish monks went up to Lindisfarne and Melrose and taught the Saxon youth and when a Saint Cuthbert and a Saint Eata repaid their charitable toil! O blessed days of peace and confidence when the Celtic Maeldub penetrated to Malmesbury in the south, which has inherited his name, and founded there the famous school which gave birth to the great Saint Aldhelm. O

Facing page and above: little fishing vessels, dwarfed by the great Atlantic trawlers, lie in Killybegs harbour. Above left: wind-tossed surf on the Inishowen Peninsula and (left) a calmer day near Greencastle.

Around Mulroy Bay (below right) lie woodlands full of lonely caves. Below left: a sandbar forms a sharp bend in the River Erne and (bottom) surf surrounds Torneady Point, Aran Island. Facing page: Dawros Head.

precious seal and testimony of Gospel unity when, as Aldhelm in turn tells us, the English went to Ireland "numerous as bees"; when the Saxon Saint Egbert and Saint Willibrord, preachers to the heathen Frisians, made the voyage to Ireland to prepare themselves for their work; and when from Ireland went forth to Germany the two noble Ewalds, Saxons also, to earn the crown of martyrdom. Such a period, indeed, so rich in peace, in love, could last only for a season.'

Not only did Irish monks have considerable influence in Scotland and Britain, but they were also renowned throughout France. Brittany was one of their first ports of call. Forever associated with the conversion of the Bretons – themselves fellow Celts – are Saint Ronan and Saint Sithney. Saint Ronan was a bishop who had worked in Cornwall, also part of the pan-Celtic culture, and he is buried in Locronan. Saint Sithney is

'The great waves of the Atlantic sweep storming on their way,
Shining green and silver with the hidden herring shoal,
But the little waves of Breffny have drenched my heart in spray,
And the little waves of Breffny go stumbling through my soul.'

(Eva Gore-Booth 1870-1926)

□

Right: cows grazing on one of the many drumlins comprising Cavan. Cavan is the most southerly of the nine counties of the Province of Ulster. It is a land of myriad lakes, including Lough Ramar (below).

associated with Brittany, where he is said to have landed with seventy disciples. He built a monastery at Guisseny and ministered to the people of Leon there. He died in the year 530. There is a Breton folk tale about him which said that the Lord wanted him to become the patron saint of girls. He was horrified at the thought, as he could see himself being besieged by young ladies looking for husbands and dowries, so he asked if he could be made the patron saint of mad dogs instead. His reasoning was that it would be easier to look after mad dogs than women.

The Irish Saint Tresan is the patron saint of the Champagne district. He, and his three sisters and six brothers, settled in Chalons-sur-Marne at the beginning of the fifth century, and there was great devotion to him in Rheims.

In the sixth century the Irish Saint Frindolin became abbot of the monastery at Poiters. He was very much a wanderer, and after discovering the relics of Saint Hilary, he built a church in the saint's honour. He wandered through Alsace-Lorraine, Burgundy, Switzerland and Austria, living for a time on an island in the Rhine, and founding the monastery at Sackingen near Basle.

The Irish abbot and saint, Fursey, who died in 650, joined the wanderers for Christ by going to East Anglia, where he founded his first monastery in the old fort of Cnobheresburg, given to him by the local King Sigebert, which we now know as Burg Castle in Suffolk. When Sigebert was killed in battle, Fursey moved to France. While on a pilgrimage to Rome he paused at Picardy, and the local ruler there, Erchinoald, was so moved by his miracles that he granted him land on which to build a monastery at Lagny-sur-Marne. Saint Fursey died in the area of the Somme and was buried in Péronne. According to the Venerable Bede, the miracle worker Fursey was one of the first saints to be granted visions of Hell and Heaven, and was one of the first to warn sinners about the punishments in store for them.

Two disciples of Saint Fursey, saints Gobain and Algis, carried on his work. Saint Gobain became famous as a hermit in the region of Laon, and Saint Algis was befriended by King Clovis and set up a monastery at Mont-Saint-Julien on the River Oise. Today there is a town and a forest named after Saint Gobain.

Above: a Cavan man and his Morris Minor. At Cuilcagh Lough
Dean Swift wrote *Gulliver's Travels* and from Cavan came William
James, the grandfather of the novelist, Henry James.

Saint Fiacre, another Irish monk self-exiled for the sake of Christ around the year 630, came to Meaux where, along with his companion Saint Kilian, he was welcomed by Bishop Faro. Saint Kilian went to live at Aubigny, and Saint Fiacre set up as a hermit at Breuil, near Meaux. He built a hostel for pilgrims, and thousands of people, ranging from kings to peasants, beat a path to his door. There was enormous devotion to him throughout France from the sixth until the twelfth century, and his name is still invoked in France today. As he was an expert gardener he became the patron saint of horticulturalists, but also achieved fame as a saint who could cure venereal disease. There was a hotel in Paris named after him, the Hotel Saint Fiacre. In the seventeenth century, an astute business man with a devotion to him set up a coach hire company, calling the carriages 'Saint Fiacre'. Rapidly these horse-drawn carriages for hire became referred to as 'fiacres', and some French taxi-cabs still retain this name today. At the height of his devotional fame, Saint Fiacre was revered by Queen Anne of Austria, Louis XIII and Saint Vincent de Paul. His fame has since spread to the Netherlands and Germany. He is buried in Meaux.

Above left: sunset over Lower Lough Erne and (above and left) views towards Lower Lough Erne from Lough Navar Forest. The River Erne dominates the entire County of Fermanagh in this, the 'Lakelands' of Ireland – a boating and fishing paradise. Facing page: Inner Lake in Dartry Forest.

'No more thy glassy brook reflects the day,
But, choked with sedges, works its weedy way
Along thy glades, a solitary guest,
The hollow-sounding bittern guards its nest;
Amidst thy desert walks the lapwing flies,
And tires their echoes with unvaried cries.
Sunk are thy bowers, in shapeless ruin all,
And the long grass o'ertops the mouldering wall,
And, trembling, shrinking from the spoiler's hand,
Far, far away, thy children leave the land.'

(Oliver Goldsmith 1730-1774)

☐
Above: the ruins of the
Old Hall, once the site of
the palace of the
O'Rourkes, at Dromahair.
Right: Carrick-on-
Shannon, where the
fishing is reputed to be
extremely good.

The tradition of Irish saints in France was to continue long after Saint Fiacre. In the twelfth century, Saint Laurence O'Toole, Abbot of Glendalough and Archbishop of Dublin (consecrated in Christchurch Cathedral on the hill of Dublin in 1162), was to die in Eu, becoming known in France as Saint Laurent d'Eu, in Seine-Inferieure. After the death of Saint Laurence on 14th November, 1180, his tomb immediately became a centre of popular pilgrimage, so much so that a large church had to be built and his body placed in its crypt. He was canonized in Rome by Pope Honorius III in 1225, and pilgrims still crowd to his shrine.

Above: a cowhand who prefers a bicycle to a horse. Right: a waterfall in the Glencar Lakes district (far right). County Leitrim is the county of the clan O'Rourke.

□
Right: a plume of steam
marks Lanesborough's
peat-burning power
station. Below: St Mel's
Cathedral, Longford City,
whose appearance belies
its nineteenth-century
date.

Right: the entrance hall in Clonalis House, a house of mementoes of the O'Connor Don family that span 1,500 years of Irish history. Below: Lough Key and (below right) Roscommon, which can boast a fifteenth-century Dominican friary and a thirteenth-century castle.

Saint Laurence (or Lorcan) O'Toole has a very special place in the affections of the Irish. Born in County Kildare, he was of royal lineage, the son of the chief of the O'Toole clan. In his youth he was held as a hostage by the treacherous King of Leinster, Diarmuid McMurrough. He joined the monastery of Glendalough, some thirty miles south of Dublin, and was made the abbot there at the young age of twenty-five. He was elected Archbishop of Dublin in 1162 and, as such, was in a difficult position when the Norman-English invaded Ireland. Henry II was claiming Ireland as part of his kingdom, and was infuriated by the visit to Rome of Laurence O'Toole, who gave Pope Alexander a full report of political events in Ireland. Made a papal legate, the Saint procured papal protection for much of the property of the See of Dublin, and Glendalough. The high King of Ireland, Rory O'Connor, was on his way out as the Norman church

Below: Athlone market. Athlone, birthplace of John McCormack, the tenor, is the chief market town of Westmeath. The town marks the dividing line between the provinces of Leinster and Connacht. Facing page: flat tyre.

take-over began under Henry II. The King, furious with the independence shown by the saint in Rome, refused to see him when he called on him at Abingdon in England. Undaunted, the Saint followed Henry II to Normandy. It was on his way back to Dublin that he died in exile in Eu.

There is an extraordinary 'presence' of Irish monks in parts of France today which can be sensed in towns like Péronne, whose streets were once embarrassingly crowded with wandering Irish monk-scholars. We know, for example that the *episcopi et sacerdotes vagantes*, like the travelling people, the tinkers of our day, were becoming such a nuisance in France and Europe that at the Council of Soissons in 744 Saint Boniface called for stern measures to be taken to bring them into line. Later, in the

Almost at Ireland's centre, Athlone (above) is a meeting place for
road, rail and river.

☐
Castle Mound (right), near the church in Clonard, is generally considered to be sepulchral. Below: The Three Jolly Pigeons bar, and (below right) rowing boats in late afternoon sunshine.

reign of the scholarly lover of learning, Charles the Bald, the Irish monks gathered in large numbers in Soissons to discuss language and literature. The son of Charles the Bald, Carolman, joined the Irish monks in the monastery they had set up in Soissons in the ninth century. This centre of learning produced the greatest Irish philosopher of all time, John Scottus Eriugena.

Similarly, in Reims, the Irish monk-scholars set up shop with the help of Pippin the Short, the monk Donatus becoming Archbishop of Reims. Metz was another centre of Irish scholarship. Irish monks were so much in favour with the local bishops that the Emperor Otto III was persuaded to issue a special charter on their behalf in 992. It read:

'It is directed that the first abbot, an Irishman named Fingenius, who has now been installed there by the above-mentioned bishop, (the bishop of Metz) and his successors, shall receive Irish monks as long as such is possible. Should monks from Ireland fail there, the number of inmates is always to be maintained by recruits of other nationalities.'

There are many young men of distinguished families in Ireland today who rejoice in the Christian name of Fursey, after the Irish abbot who, as we have already seen, helped convert East Anglia, and then converted the French in the region of the Marne and the Somme. Less well known today, and rare as a Christian name, is the brother of Saint Fursey, Saint Foillan. Saint Foillan (or Faelan) had helped his brother, Fursey, found the abbey in East Anglia. When the King of Mercia's men destroyed the abbey, Saint Foillan headed for the Continent, and was martyred in Belgium, where he

□

Above: a pony helps to plough a steep Laois field in a county known for its limestone hills. Right: the view from the Rock of Dunamase, near Portlaoise.

Below: a Laois farmhouse stands amid harvested wheat fields
below the Rock of Dunamase.

is known as Saint Pholien. With his brother he had been well received by
Clovis II, and founded a monastery at Fosses on land granted to him by
the Abbess of Nivelles, Abbess Ita. His cause is well known today in the
Brabant, while Ita is no less well known as a remarkably generous and
able woman who served the poor and fed and sheltered travellers in the
region. Saint Foillan spent much of his time visiting the Irish monasteries,
such as Peronne and Laquy, and it was while he was on one of these visits
that he was assassinated by robbers at Serette, who cut off his head and
buried his body in a ditch. The nuns led prayers for the recovery of his
body, and it is said that it was found on the anniversary of the death of his
brother, Fursey. He was buried at the monastery of Fosses in 655.

His monastery today is a parish church, where the Belgian tourist
authorities are happy to see over 50,000 people attend the Festival of
Saint Foillan, which is held every seventh year. It is the greatest folk
festival in Belgium, during which his relics are carried with all due pomp
and circumstance around the former boundaries of his monastery.
Villages for miles around send volunteers in historic military costumes to
accompany them and a *feu-de-joie* is fired at intervals in salute to an Irish
saint who, rather ironically, is virtually unknown in Ireland.

Clonmacnoise (above), on the banks of the Shannon four miles
from Shannonbridge, is one of the most celebrated monastic
foundations in Ireland. Founded by St Ciaran, it dates from 548.

The remarkable Saint Gertrude (not the 'Great' Saint Gertrude, who was a Benedictine visionary of the 13th century), who had the prayers said for the recovery of the body of Saint Foillan, had established – on typically Irish lines – double monasteries, one for men and one for women, which were constructed as those first set out by Saint Brigid of Kildare. Near Fosses is a church dedicated to Saint Brigid, and it is still a popular centre of pilgrimage on her feast day, 1st February. Brigid of Kildare died in 525, since which the devotion of her following has achieved parity with that of the Apostle of Ireland, Saint Patrick himself. Of humble origin – she was a slave girl who tended cows – she rapidly became a cult figure in Britain and throughout the Continent, founded the first convent in Ireland and became the patron saint of poets, healers and blacksmiths. Of the several

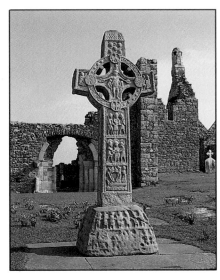

□
Left: the Clonmacnoise South Cross and (above) an early Christian stone nearby. Top: Catholic prayers.

Left: the archway to the Nuns' Church at Clonmacnoise (bottom). Below: horse-drawn timber.

dozen churches dedicated to her in Britain alone, the most famous is St Brides, the church of journalists in London's Fleet Street. With its tall, ornate steeple it became 'the bride's church'; the tiers of wedding cakes today feature its steeple.

Saint Brigid is revered all over Europe: the farmers of Liège in France built a church in her honour, looking to her as the protector of their agricultural lands. Due to her origins, she was the Irish saint most associated with cows in the byre, and her blessings are invoked on all the places on a farm, particularly where mucking-out takes place.

Another Irish saint associated with Belgium who became a cult figure in Europe is Saint Dympna, a martyr. For some she is associated with the ancient kingdom of Oriel, once in County Monaghan, an undulating land of great beauty. Tydavnit, just four miles northwest of Monaghan town, is presumed to be named (in Irish) after Saint Damhnait, or Dympna. She was a daughter of the sixth-century King of Oriel, an incestuous pagan. The accepted story is that her mother died when she was a very small child and she grew up to look exactly like her. Her incestuous father fell in love with her and, to escape his unwelcome attentions, she ran away with her confessor, Saint Gerebernus, to Antwerp, and lived as a hermit at Gheel, some twenty-five miles from there. The King followed her, failed to persuade her to return to Ireland, and so personally killed her confessor. In medieval times she became the patroness of the insane and epileptics, and many miraculous cures were attributed to her intercession. Gradually the town of Gheel, where her body was buried in the church named after her, became a centre of pilgrimage. The townspeople made a special point of looking after the insane and the mentally ill, and Gheel is still, in our time, noted for its mental hospital. The town's medieval statue of Saint Dympna shows the young saint holding the Devil of Insanity in check. On her feast day, 15th May, the town goes *en fête*, and her relics are carried in a solemn procession around the town square, attracting thousands of pilgrims and tourists.

Irish singing pubs, such as J. J. Hough's Pub (above) at Banagher, are of two varieties. There are the obvious tourist traps, where bleary-eyed tenors abound, and then there are those where the Irish go.

Below: resting from their labours, two turf cutters silhouetted
against the sunset in a county with a substantial acreage of peat
bog (facing page).

Flemish-speaking Belgians revere the memory of the Irish saint, Livinius of
Ghent, who was martyred in 660 by pagans at Saint Lievem-Houten. The
most popular Irish monk-scholar in Belgium was Sedulius Scottus of
Liège. The local bishop, Hartgar, put him in charge of the cathedral
school. Like many ninth-century Irish scholars, Sedulius Scottus was a
man versed in Greek, and also a theologian, a poet and a philosopher of
universal excellence. He gathered other Irish scholars of note around him,
and they produced collections of tracts and manuscripts. Sedulius is best
known for his work *De Rectoribus Christianis*, a guide for kings wishing to
rule as Christians. Liège became a popular 'clearing house' for Irish
scholars on the move through Europe in the ninth century, and there was
also a famous Irish monastery fairly close by in the forests of the
Ardennes, the Abbey of Waulsort, the abbot of which was
inevitably an Irishman.

In Germany the earliest Irish monks were up against an ultra-barbaric,
pagan, forest-dwelling people quite unlike the French, who burnt
prisoners in iron cages over a slow fire, worshipping gods such as Wodan.
They believed that all warriors who died in battle entered the Hall of
Valhalla, their heaven. According to Cornelius Tacitus (56-117), the
Roman historian, in his *Germanica*, the Germans were totally separated
from the rest of Europe by the Rhine, the Danube and the Black Forest.
Pure Nordics, with blue eyes, red hair and large frames, they did not marry
foreigners, and human sacrifice was common. The Romans feared the
Germans and in fact lost five armies to them, so powerful and seemingly
inhuman were they in battle.

Right: a dilapidated sash window provides a cat with a place to sun itself. Below: Kinvarra and Kinvarra Bay, south of Galway city, and (bottom) some of the famous Twelve Bens of Connemara. The county is, in part, still Gaelic-speaking.

Galway (below left and below right) was the setting for John
Ford's film, *The Quiet Man*. Clifden (bottom), boasting a double-
spired church, is the 'capital' of Connemara – the most beautiful
part of Galway.

Yet before we follow in the footsteps of the Irish monk-scholars of
Germany, it is interesting to note that the German village of Hohenstadt in
Baden-Wuerttemberg has been devoted to Saint Patrick for some six
hundred years. The quaint statue of a young, clean-shaven Saint Patrick in
the parish church shows him in his conventional mitre, holding his
pectoral cross in one hand and a missal in the other. Like Saint Brigid,
Saint Patrick of Hohenstadt achieved fame as a protector of cattle from
disease. There are said to be relics of the saint in the church in
Hohenstadt, a claim which is quite unique. On the feast of Saint Patrick
several thousand pilgrims take part in a solemn high mass and procession
in his honour. This is one of the rare places in Germany where local boys
are given the name Patrick in baptism. Indeed, one of the extraordinary
facts about the Irish monk-scholar invasion of Germany is that it produced
150 patron saints in villages and towns throughout Germany who are

The curragh (above) is a traditional boat crafted for the Atlantic,
but so light that two men can put it on their shoulders and carry it
to the sea. Facing page: (top) the Hooker Races, Carna, and
(bottom) Galway people.

virtually unknown in Ireland or anywhere else. As a German bishop once remarked to Daniel O'Connell (who won emancipation for the Irish and English Catholics in 1829):

'We can never forget to look upon your beloved country as our mother in religion. Ireland, in the remotest periods of the Christian era, sent forth her sons to rescue our pagan ancestors from idolatry.'

Another German writer, speaking almost a hundred years later, said,

'The Celts with their weakly natures had no inclination for firm organisation – a gentle, rather sentimental people who could manage nothing more than the co-operation of those in perfect unison, which became the first step in an organised church'.

☐ Roundstone harbour (right and below right) lies on the western side of Bertraghboy Bay. It is well-sheltered, being almost land-locked, and is set amid some of the finest scenery in Connemara.

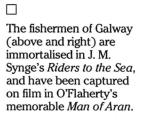 The fishermen of Galway (above and right) are immortalised in J. M. Synge's *Riders to the Sea*, and have been captured on film in O'Flaherty's memorable *Man of Aran*.

Below: the masts of fishing boats in Roundstone harbour point
towards the blue-green bulk of the Connemara mountains.

The early Irish monks and scholars in Germany tended to be hermits and led many pagan people to Christianity, as Christ did, by the example of the perfection of their daily lives. There were also typical vagrant Irish priests and bishops in Germany. It was on their informal foundations that one of the greatest English saints of all time, Saint Boniface, set up formal ecclesiastical patterns there, with dioceses in submission to the central authority of Rome. It could be safely reckoned that any German who had a knowledge of Greek at this time had been taught by Irish monks.

For centuries the Irish people have been loyal in their faith to Rome, but, at the same time, frequently sceptical of its politics. Like the Poles, they took their religion from Rome, but regarded politics as their own business. A classic example of the inept political attitude which the Vatican could adopt regarding Ireland was given by Pope Alexander VIII in the seventeenth century. He had St Peters outlined with massive celebratory

It is still possible to draw water from the village pump (below) in
Galway. Facing page: watching the boats return to Killary Harbour.

candles, and a solemn *Te Deum* sung in thanksgiving for the victory of the
Protestant King William of Orange over the Catholic King James at the
Battle of the Boyne in Ireland. It suited the political policy of the Pope at
the time, which was to support the Protestant cause against the
Gallicanism of Louis XIV of France.

Probably the first Irish monk on the German scene was seventh-century
Saint Frindolin, who established a monastery at Seckingen on an island in
the Rhine. In the early stages of the progress towards Christianising
Germany, Irish monks were liable to be unpopular – or even murdered, as

□

Right: hand-rearing sheep on a smallholding near Leenane (below right), an attractive angling centre at the head of Killary Harbour.

□

Above: Ballynahinch Lake in Connemara, renowned for the good fishing it provides. Right: Lough Corrib, the second largest lake in Ireland, whose northern shores are bounded by Joyce Country.

Saint Kilian was for denouncing the incestuous marriage of the Duke of Gozbert's wife. The Emperor Otto III had a soft spot for Irish scholars: they were given care of the church of Saint Pantaleon in Cologne and were made more than welcome everywhere: indeed, the monastery of Saint Martin in Cologne had Irish abbots in charge of it from 975 to 1061; Marianus Scottus, who lived there from 1056 to 1058, gave all their names in his *Chronicle* of the Abbey.

Saint Fintan of Rheinau was born in Leinster. He was captured in a Viking raid, escaped in the Orkneys and, in thanksgiving, made a pilgrimage to Rome. On the journey back, he joined a group of fellow Irish hermits in their monastery on an island in the Rhine at Theinau, near Schaffhausen. He spent twenty-two years in voluntary solitary confinement in his cell in this monastery, dying in 879. His relics are in Rheinau.

In the sixth century at Säckingen, south of the Black Forest, the Irish saint and abbot, Frindolin, founded his monastery just down the Rhine from Rheinau and also founded a nunnery. He had a reputation as a sportsman,

The Twelve Bens of Connemara (above) occupy a circle some five miles in diameter and tower above the surrounding landscape. They include the conical peaks, all over 2,000 feet high, of Benbaum, Bencorr and Bencollaghduff.

encouraging sport among the postulant monks. He settled down at Säckingen after wandering from Ireland to Northumbria, and from there to France. He has a large following in Austria and in Switzerland, as well as in Southern Germany, and his relics are enshrined in the local church. Many farmers revere him as a patron saint of their farm animals, particularly of horned cattle and horses, and there is an annual pilgrimage in his honour on 6th March.

☐

Green fields (facing page) marked by drystone walls, such as those near Roundstone (right), are typical of Galway. Below: the road to Leenane in the Maamturk Mountains. Bottom: Dawros River rushes past a deserted croft, and (bottom right) a haystack nears completion.

Left: the drowned valley of Killary Harbour on the Galway-Mayo border. Extending inland for some eight miles, this is one of the loveliest inlets on the Irish coast. Above and top: Galway farmers.

The Galway Races (this page) are usually held at the end of July and attract thousands of punters from all over Ireland. Being a two-day flat-racing classic, the festivities usually last for at least seven days.

Below: bookies consider their profits at the Galway Races. Over four million pounds in bets is said to change hands during this festival of the Irish thoroughbred.

The most celebrated Irish saint in Austria is Saint Coleman, from County Cork. His tomb is in the famous Benedictine Abbey of Melk, on the banks of the River Danube. He was on his way to the Holy Land when he was killed by the men of Stockerau, near Vienna, in 1012. The cult of Coleman spread rapidly all over southern Germany, Austria and Hungary. He is invoked for a blessing of healing for farm horses, and for centuries on Whit Monday people would take their horses to a chapel built in his honour near Wurtemberg. Bavarians too have an annual blessing of cattle and horses in his name at Hohenschwangan.

Saint Pirmin, who died in 753, was a wanderer, and therefore probably Irish, and he founded the monastery of Reichenau. He assembled a considerable library, and his monastery became a focal point for Irish monks. He was the author of *Dicta Pirimini*, one of the earliest popular works of theology against prevalant superstitions. The present day diocese of Salzburg abounds in the remains of eighth-century churches erected by early Irish saints, including the church at Wilparting, where two Irish saints are buried, Saint Makin and Saint Anian, are buried.

The pilgrim path of Irish monks in Ratisbon led to Russia and as far as Kiev. The monks asked the King of Bohemia for assistance in providing them with an escort on this perilous journey. This was forthcoming, and

☐
These pages: the Galway Races. For some reason best known to Irish race-goers, Irish bookies are known as 'turf accountants'. They have nothing to do with the turf that is dug from the bog for fuel, but are instead very concerned with the 'going' on the green sod – the hallowed ground of Irish racetracks.

an Irish monk, Maurice, returned loaded with gifts of Russian furs, the sale of which went towards the building of the Abbey of Saint James at Ratisbon. Gradually and naturally the Irish monks in Germany, who had made thousands of converts, were replaced by German monks. Such was the case in the Benedictine monastery of Nürnberg, founded in 1140, and this also happened in the Benedictine monastery at Erfurt, founded in the twelfth century. Saint Bernard, speaking of these Irish monks referred to them as *'examina sanctorum'*, 'a swarm of saints' spreading out through Europe.

Top: late afternoon sun warms the land near Maam Cross in Connemara (above right). Above left: Killary Harbour, which is nowhere much more than half-a-mile wide. Facing page: sunburst over Slyne Head.

'The wing is our confederate
The night has left her doors ajar,
We meet beyond earth's barréd gate
Where all the world's wild Rebels are.'

(Eva Gore-Booth 1870-1926)

Right: fly-fishing in Galway. Fishing is probably the most popular sport in Ireland, the rivers, lakes and coastline catering for all types of anglers. Lough Corrib in County Galway is one of the largest fishing centres in the West. Below: an innovative sign for one of Inishbofin's famed seafood restaurants.

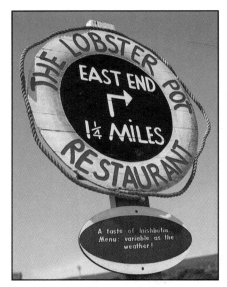

Left: pipe-making near Leenane and (above) young Galway hurling players resting a while from their game.

The bodhrán (left) is a frame drum made from goat skin. The treated skin is tacked under tension to its beechwood frame and the resulting drum or 'tamb', is beaten with a small stick. Below: a young Gaelic football team.

From the time of Charles the Great Irish monk scholars were moving through Italy and teaching at the monastery of Saint Augustine in Pavia. Saint Fridian, an Irish monk-bishop, led a hermit's life on Monte Pisano near Lucca, and was buried in the Church of Saint Fridian of Lucca in 588. His remains lie beneath the high altar. Tuscany was to see several dozen churches under his patronage, including some in Florence and Pisa. Fiesole, so near to Florence, is associated with the great Irish saint, Donatus, who was made bishop by popular demand in 829. His relics are in the cathedral there today. As a scholar he is remembered for his poetic life of Saint Brigid and a Latin poem about his native land.

☐ Aran Island fields (this page) contain earth comprised of a mixture of sand and seaweed. Ireland's earliest Christian hermits settled on these islands in beehive-shaped cells.

Right: the bleak limestone cliffs of Inishmore, the largest of the Aran Islands of Galway Bay. In response to such an inhospitable environment, the islanders created the magnificent Aran Isle sweater. In its true form, this woollen is virtually waterproof. Below: Dun Aengus, a pre-Christian monument considered one of the finest in Europe. Below right: Inisheer, the smallest of the three islands.

A seventh-century Irish saint, Cathaldus of Taranto is known throughout Southern Italy and Sicily – his silver statue stands in the cathedral of Saint Cathaldus today and a large statue of him overlooks the port of Taranto. Cathaldus was born in the province of Munster and studied at the monastic school of Lismore, on the banks of the River Blackwater in County Waterford. It is probable that his Irish name, Cathal, was Latinised as 'Cathaldus'. There are churches and chapels dedicated to him in Modena, Cremona, Venice, Bologna, Rimini and Bari, as well as in Palermo

☐
Right: the traditional
curragh in use on a
gently sloping beach
(below) in the Aran
Islands.

☐
Above right: a horse and
trap pause by a water
pump in Kilronan, the
capital of Inishmore.
Right: Dungory Castle, at
the head of Kinvarra Bay.

Below: weathered faces, strong arms and great courage – the marks of Aran men.

and Nicosia, also in Sicily. Forever revered in Malta, he is the patron saint to have recourse to in times of storms, plagues and droughts. He was shipwrecked in the Bay of Taranto on his way back from a pilgrimage to the Holy Land. In the bay, surprisingly enough, the locals will point out to you 'L'Anello di San Cataldo', the bubbling spring of fresh water that marks the spot where he threw his episcopal ring into the sea to quell a violent storm. There is also a miraculous well on the shore near Taranto which is named after him and has curative powers. When his coffin was discovered in Taranto in 1071, his Celtic-designed crozier was found beside his incorrupt body. During the Second World War he became the patron saint of Italian soldiers.

If we search the mass of Irish manuscripts in the museums, libraries and monasteries of Germany today, somewhere we will find that one of the early Irish scholar monks put quill to parchment and wrote down, for the first time, the legend that when Saint Patrick fasted for forty days and forty nights on Croagh Patrick, Ireland's holy mountain, he wrested from God the right to judge the Irish on the Day of Judgement. If this be the case, then when the Irish saints go marching in, the Saint should see among the leaders such miracle workers and healers as Fr John Sullivan S.J. (1861-1933), the mystic Fr Willy Doyle S.J., M.C. (1873-1917), a chaplain blown to pieces on the Western front line on 16th August 1917 while ministering to his wounded men, and then Edel Quinn, the saintly young woman of the Legion of Mary, born in 1907, who died in Nairobi on the African Mission in 1944. The more the Irish *peregrini* are studied the more it becomes evident that the old saying is so very true, namely that a

☐
When Irish people say the word 'Mayo', they usually add, half jokingly, 'God help us', as it is a county which has had a very sad, harsh and hungry history. Above: a donkey, a typical beast of burden in Ireland, helps with the haymaking on the shores of Lough Conn (left).

prophet is seldom honoured in his own country. It has also been sagely
remarked that an Irishman is never so much at home as
when he is abroad.

A paradox within the story of the Irish saints is the fact that, while they
numbered hundreds in Ireland's Golden Age, only four have ever been
formally canonised by Rome, and only one of these – Saint Virgil of
Salzburg – was actually from the Golden Age. Even Saint Malachy,
Archbishop of Armagh (who lived between 1094 and 1148) was never
formally declared a saint by Rome, although Pope Clement III approved of

□
Above: a good crop of
hay on the banks of
Lough Conn, near
Crossmolina. Typically,
County Mayo is a land of
bleak moorlands and
long sandy beaches. Left:
the ruins of Rosserk
Abbey overlook the
estuary of the River Moy
in northern Mayo.

an already existing devotion to him among Cistercian monks, and much was made of the fact that this reforming Archbishop died in exile, on his *ad limina* visit to Rome, in the arms of the Great Saint Bernard of Clairvaux. As we have seen, the twelfth-century Archbishop of Dublin, Laurence O'Toole was canonized by Pope Honorius in 1225.

On the way to being declared a saint is Blessed Fr Charles Meehan (1640 - 1679) – an Irish Franciscan beatified in 1987 by Pope John Paul II as one of the eighty-five martyrs of the British Isles to be declared 'beati'. He was

☐
Facing page and right: the superb, twelfth-century abbey at Cong. Turlough Abbey has a round tower (above) stouter and lower than any other ninth-century round tower in Ireland. It stands on the site of a church founded by St Patrick.

As in Holland and other civilized countries of the world, the
bicycle is a nationwide mode of transport in Ireland, particularly
in rural areas (above). Facing page: (top left) Asleagh Falls near
Leenane, (top right) Kingstown Bay and (bottom) Westport, a
town divided by the Carrowbeg River.

arrested when his ship was wrecked in the Irish Sea, and he was forced ashore in Wales. He was hanged, drawn and quartered at Ruthin in 1679, his 'crime' being that he was a seminary priest within the jurisdiction of Rome. He had, in fact, been on his way back from Rome at the time of the shipwreck.

Considering how great the contribution of the Irish Church has been to the Church of Rome, it has been much overlooked and its saints generally taken for granted. In fact, the Polish Pope, John Paul II, who visited Ireland en route to the United States in 1979, was the first pope in history to bestow any sort of recognition on the Irish for their loyalty to the Supreme Pontiff in Rome.

In the race for Irish saints in modern times, Saint Oliver Plunket, an aristocratic Archbishop of Armagh, was the Establishment's favourite for canonisation, so he was 'first past the post' by a long way – a spiritual case of 'Hyperion first and the rest nowhere'. A martyr, he was the last Catholic to be executed at Tyburn in London in 1681 and was canonized in 1976. In the canonisation stakes the clergy are a money-on bet – the laity are way down the field. Hot on the heels of Saint Oliver Plunkett is

Facing page: (top left) Black Sod Point, (top right) Achill Head and (bottom) Killary Harbour. Clew Bay (above) is an expanse of the Atlantic Ocean that embraces scores of tiny islands. Left: spring tides at Downpatrick, north Mayo.

The most famous feature of the county is Croagh Patrick, Patrick's Mountain, which rises 2,500 feet above the shore and islands of Clew Bay (below). Here St Patrick is said to have fasted for forty days and wrestled with the Devil.

the founder of the Irish Christian Brothers, Edmond Ignatius Rice of Waterford, a married man who, when his wife died, established the Brothers for the Christian Education of Youth in Ireland. He died in 1844, and his brothers in religion have a strong lobby going for him in Rome.

Way down the field today is a one-time favourite is Matt Talbot, an ex-alcholic, Dublin working man, who lived between 1850 and 1925 and is now regarded as a 'servant of God'. If ever a man had the Devil riding on his back, it was he. Matt the mystic, product of the stinking tenements of Dublin, collapsed and died in a city back street called Granby Lane. On his arrival in Jervis Street Hospital his frail, starved body was found to be bound with penitential chains. Clearly the Vatican of today has yet to see its way to proclaiming an ex-lush Dublin worker-in-chains, a saint of temperance, a saint for our times.

The great strength in the combination of dream and reality in Celtic life was outlined by the poet and writer, Lord Dunsany, a Meath man. He said:

One of the chastening experiences for a young man climbing the 'Rock', Croagh Patrick, on the annual pilgrimage (this page), is to be passed by barefoot old ladies. Such is their devotion that they pay scant heed to their bruised and bleeding feet.

Croaghpatrick Pilgrimage

Every pilgrim who ascends the mountain on St. Patrick's Day or within the octave, or any time during the months of June, July, August and September, and PRAYS IN OR NEAR THE CHAPEL for the intentions of our Holy Father the Pope may gain a plenary indulgence on condition of going to Confession and Holy Communion on the Summit or within the week.

THE TRADITIONAL STATIONS

There are three "stations": (1) At the base of the cone or Leacht Benain, (2) On the summit, (3) Roilig Muire, some distance down the Lecanvey side of the mountain.

1st Station — LEACHT BENAIN

The pilgrim walks seven times around the mound of stones saying seven Our Fathers, seven Hail Marys and one Creed.

2nd Station — THE SUMMIT

(a) The pilgrim kneels and says 7 Our Fathers, 7 Hail Marys and one Creed.
(b) The pilgrim prays near the Chapel for the Pope's intentions.
(c) The pilgrim walks 15 times around the Chapel saying 15 Our Fathers, 15 Hail Marys and one Creed.
(d) The pilgrim walks 7 times around Leaba Phadraig saying 7 Our Fathers, 7 Hail Marys and one Creed.

3rd Station — ROILIG MUIRE

The pilgrim walks 7 times around each mound of stones saying 7 Our Fathers 7 Hail Marys and one Creed at each and finally goes around the whole enclosure of Roilig Muire 7 times praying.

When you ascend St Patrick's Mountain in the company of fellow pilgrims, there is a carnival atmosphere – as well as an air of competition to see who gets to the top first.

For the mere male it is chastening to see the number of young and not-so-young ladies (these pages) who climb Croagh Patrick at a steady pace, calmly, purposefully and without a care in the world. It can be truly said that they have the Faith.

'Christ of the supper room,
Christ of the empty tomb,
Christ of the Day of Doom
In the White Host.'

(Roibéard O Faracháin)

Ashford Castle (these pages) was formerly the county seat of the Guinness family. Here they entertained English royalty in style, including one famous honeymoon couple.

Ashford Castle has won international awards as a hotel – one of which declared it to be the best in Europe. Its distinguished guest list includes President Nixon and President Reagan.

'The real Ireland is a land of dreams. It is for the sake of the dream that we send ministers to Poland and Ruritania, for the sake of the dream that we have a Minister of External Affairs, and keep an army. And if we are not looking at the stars as we walk, or looking for them at broad noon, we are looking back over our shoulders at what has gone ages since, and peering back even further through the mist and the haze of Time, to see bright and clear in the radiance that shines from our vivid dreams, the kings and the heroes of days that never were. And that we shall part with last of all.

No nation shall take from us our myths and our fables; no man shall prove that our demi-gods did not live: we would as soon give up St Patrick as give up the snakes he expelled. And why? Because St Patrick was real,

Below right and below left: Downpatrick Head. Bottom: Westport
Bay, near Murrisk, part of far larger Clew Bay.

and can look after himself. But the Irish snakes never lived, and so they
need our support. They need it, and they shall have it. In stone and on
parchment and on whatever craftsmen can ornament, long snakes with
crocodile's jaws make our favourite design. In England men are proud to
protect the weak, but that is scarcely knightly enough for us: we protect
the non-existent. While an Irishman lives to defend them no phoenix will
die, no leprechaun, no fairy. And as for our ancient kings and the gods of
old and the demi-gods, to them our allegiance goes out; and we are less
likely to forsake one of them for anything modern, than for the discovery
of some still older Irish demi-god.'

St Patrick, the mystic, the visionary, was a Briton, and a modern British
visionary, the poet and writer Gilbert Keith Chesterton, had this
experience to relate as he left the shores of Ireland after his
first visit in 1918:

'As new lengths of coast and lines of heights were unfolded, I had the
fancy that the whole land was not receding but advancing, like something
spreading out its arms to the world … I remembered that the men of this
island had once gone forth, not with torches of conqueror destroyers, but
as missionaries in the very midnight of the Dark Ages; like a multitude of
moving candles, that were the light of the world.'

Above: Lough Conn, a lough well known to fishermen. It was here
that a record-sized pike, weighing fifty-three pounds, was caught
in 1920.

☐

Right: Lough Conn, large enough to take a fleet of boats, none of which will see more than a glimpse of any other until their homecoming in the evening.

With so many beautiful fishing loughs (top) in the West, the visiting fisherman can expect some fine catches. Above: turf cutting on the moor.

☐ Right: Drumcliff, a village beautifully situated at the mouth of the Drumcliff River. W. B. Yeats is buried in its churchyard.

☐ Above right: a Glencar waterfall and (right) Glencar Lough – in Irish, 'the Lake of the Standing Stone' – near Drumcliff, which features in the poetry of W. B. Yeats. Above: sheep and their lambs near Glencar Lough.

Benbulben (below), the 'Table Mountain' of Ireland, is the
dominant geographical feature of the region. While it is of interest
to the botanist for its rare alpine flora, it is of historical interest as
the site of the death of Diarmuid, hero of the love epic *The Pursuit
of Diarmuid and Grainne*.

A close friend of Chesterton, John Morton, a fellow Englishman and a poet
and historian, had this to say after his visit to Ireland for the
Eucharistic Congress of 1932:

'It is my purpose here merely to record a personal impression, but an
impression which has remained vivid in my mind, and which made me
realize the continuity of Ireland's history. For the new Ireland is what she
is only because she is the old Ireland. Whatever today she may be
growing into, her strong roots are in the remote past, and the philosophy
which guides her actions is the old Christian philosophy of the West. That
week of the Congress was her reply to the faint-hearted who think that
our Christendom has grown decrepit with age, and her challenge to those
who were saying that perhaps, after all, the gates of Hell shall prevail.
There in Dublin was weak faith strengthened, sick faith restored to health,
and old Europe found at her side a vigorous young champion. And at the
end of it all I had a kind of waking dream as I went about the streets at
nightfall, thinking of the light shining in the darkness from end to end of
Ireland, rows of candles and lamps set in the windows and shining out
into streets or into quiet lanes, or single flames answering each other from
remote farms or from cabins on mountainsides. *Et lux in tenebris lucet*. I
saw the whole of Ireland spread beneath the heavens like one great altar.
Or, again, I saw all those lights merged into one steady flame which was
set in a high window of the world, to bring wandering men to their home.'

Below: the beach at Moneygold, north of Grange. This county's coastline is low and boasts a plethora of sandy beaches, of which Moneygold's is typical. In the hinterland, however, are relatively high mountains, such as Benbulben (right).

☐
Above: a donkey waits patiently outside a shop in Collaney. Due to its strategic position, this town has been the scene of a number of battles. In 1599, Red Hugh O'Donnell defeated the English forces here, and in 1798 Captain Teeling helped defeat a force of English militia in the town.

Such is the demand for the coats of arms of Irish families,
particularly from Irish Americans, that a new craft of creating
heraldic plaques (above) now thrives in Ireland.